# OPHELIA WEARS BLACK

# OPHELIA WEARS BLACK

*the poetry & prose of*

SEGOVIA AMIL

OPHELIA WEARS BLACK



Segovia Amil
PO BOX 9457
Marina Del Rey, CA 90295
segoviaamilpoetry.com

Cover Art and Interior Illustrations by Segovia Amil | segoviaamilpoetry.com
Book Design, Interior Layout and Additional Artwork by Laura Pol
Photography by Laura Pol | pollaura.com

FIRST EDITION

# INDEX

# INTRODUCTION

I write to make sense of the all-consuming state of existing — to discern its shapes and its confusions. I write to make silent the sky (and then still, write of its swallows and its mournfulness, how it bellows and how it moans). I write to understand the constant hum slid between the distance of centuries, of years, of the quiet hours which are freed from language. I write until the contradictions are made clear. I write — until I am momentarily drained of my own mortality. Each day, as I author my own phantasmal world, which is the product of an inner darkness, my own fantasies, daydreams and hallucinated worlds come into being. They come bearing sacred gifts of healing and regeneration, reclaiming the truth of the soul: the magic behind all things. Each day, I find it in me to romanticize my pain and weave gold of my dark sorrows; and it is from this place I tell my tales. I write of world beyond worlds and a girl bound to darkness on a journey towards expansion, traveling with purpose from upper sky to underworld on strong wings.

It is to magic, the soul belongs — to the unearthly, the far-off, that which is unbound by time and space. The true cloak of the soul is magic — there is always more just outside this ephemeral, earthly existence. It is our duty to believe that. In a world of walking shadows and fixed darkness so complete, we must believe that.

It is through writing I have revisited the defining moments of my own life, made sense of them and turned what was once pain into poetry, into power, into magic. Within these pages are stories, myths, fantasies — quiet and internal pursuits at gripping the eventide of mystery and the unanswerable questions which cage the soul's existence. Turning the invisible into something tangible, something of reference: an enchanting, livable world full of promise. It is a road map of sorts, accompanied by its evidence of quest — proof of a small life lived in romance amidst all throes, all nuances. I have sought here, among other things, to breathe poetry and fantasy into the great darkness of certain human conditions: pain, sorrow, rage, trauma, spirit, and death — the great dark unknown, the banished corners of the unconscious, the Underworld mysteries.

The idea behind Ophelia Wears Black came to me after an odd dream:

A pair of wet soft eyes, I can only assume were my own, floating in the unbroken darkness. I could not tell if they were drifting through still water or if they were suspended, gliding, turning through space, through an untouchable dark matter. Perhaps they were trapped at the dark of the moon. I didn't know; all I knew was that they were in darkness. Surroundings were unable to be distinguished, for it is true darkness that merges — there are no shadows, neither curve nor shape. It is all-encompassing. It smothers and it chokes. I had no physical body to call my own for nothing seemed to be my own anymore. I was very much integrated with this dark — no longer a named being, no longer a creature of blood or bone but an airy, feathery thing of darkness; something unknown, something alien. Suddenly, right before me, a sphere — a dimly lit sphere, still as the night, began to take form…gleaming somewhere in the unknowable beyond.

It was as though an invisible hand began to draw on black paper (rendering, rendering) — a sphere, a beautiful white sphere, evolving, slowly coming into being. What a sight! What a beautiful and terrible sight! Life at last, taking on form — risking, showing bravery. I watched closely until the sphere came to completion. I watched as it became. I witnessed its slow birth — the birth of an incandescent, pale orb. When I thought nothing more could occur, when I was engulfed in deep feeling and taken by such rapture — two black serpents came up from behind the orb. Twisting. Gliding. Turning. Clockwise, they moved across this now permanent sphere. Their large black bodies groaning, clicking, looming within like gears in a clock. Who brought these creatures here and where had they come from? I wanted to ask, but I was a mute. I was no more than a pair of eyes, a spectator, watching like a cat. I was afraid this once untouched sphere would break from their coil, from their thick-skinned ways, but it did not. Together the sphere and serpents began to turn, in unison, in strange embrace like lovers almost, deep-sky objects — both planet and constellation reunited within an endless dark.

It was from this place that I began my search for the symbolism of such a dream. What did it all mean? A sphere, a serpent, twisting in a curious world. I looked to planets and constellations. It seemed reasonable, my only hope. Ophiuchus and Serpens. Hydra. Asclepius reviving the dead in the sky. Serpens passing through, behind Ophiuchus. Ophiuchus: the O of his name like a sphere, a shape, a planet of rings. Saturn. The Roman god Saturn. Saturnine: gloom, melancholy. Piece by piece, and rather prematurely, I did my best to string together any hint, any clue, in search of greater meaning. Despite my limited knowledge on such topics, it was the word "saturnine" which held tremendous significance. Melancholic dispositions. The Roman god Saturn, his dark side, his influence. Saturn, the unlucky star — which, as I would later learn, by way of old myths and astrology, was responsible for gloom, despair, melancholy, extreme loneliness, themes of death and yet, on the opposite end, responsible for a deepened creativity, making such a condition: a strange and unique gift. This understanding struck a chord and so I went further, to make sense of the serpents. To animal symbolism — and, as a result, to the question of its connection to Saturn.

What I found then, was a historical connection between the planet Saturn and its relation to, specifically, black snakes and other creatures of darkness: black animals like scorpions, insects and fleas, ravens and flies, nocturnal birds. From this place, an obsession grew for the symbolism and ancient history of serpents. The serpent, as many of us know, is the first we think of when we consider themes of death and rebirth as physically, the serpent holds the power to shed and renew its skin. The ancients believed that because serpents live in dark holes underground, that their homes were closer to the Underworld making the serpent the vein, or cord, between our world and the mysterious dark world beneath us. It is believed serpents hold within them the secrets of rebirth and regeneration and as creatures of darkness, undergoing death, always, to renew themselves into the new, forever, in unending cycles. Birth and death and birth and death; forever, circling like the rings of Saturn, like a dream of sphere and serpent.

To the Underworld, I thought, to go down and come out the other side, fresh as a serpent. This dream propelled me towards a few things: that I would create a fantasy, experiences, stories of a girl bound to darkness like a snake — coming apart, losing herself, traveling through her own painful experiences, her traumas, her saturnine nature and yet, renewing herself because of them, welcoming them and finally, seeing herself anew, whole, more powerful than before because of them.

Ophelia.

It should come as no surprise that the Greek female name Ophelia means "serpentine." Ophelia is the black serpent in my dream; the fearless and powerful serpent woman which sits in the belly of all women, circling her own sphere, her own phantasmal world. She is both creator and destroyer of her world. She owns her story, every part of it: her sorrow and her mournfulness, her joy and her ecstasies. She knows she cannot pass through the other side of her own Underworld without facing her darkest sides, knowing them fully, understanding them and finally, embracing them — seeing their perfection. Ophelia is that part in us which is drawn to the dark. She is a woman who is unashamed of the life she has lived as she knows each aspect of it points towards the development and evolution of her own soul. She welcomes suffering, tragedy, shame, all of life's throes as she knows she is equipped for them, was given the perfect form to take them on. She knows, as all of us should know, that she is only one who can live the life she lives. Only she can do this — the same way you and only you, no one else, can walk your own unique path and tell the story only you can tell. Ophelia dresses herself in black and goes out, into the teeming world, in search of the truth of her soul. This is her hunting dress. Ophelia wears black and black is her darkness — black is her pain, her grief, the quiet and solitary hours of her own mourning.

Each day, Ophelia puts on her black dress and descends into those dark passageways of her own being so that she may come out the other side, no longer trapped, no longer filled with shame but animated with force, magic and impenetrable spirit. Ophelia sees into the beyond. She is always with her dark, listening, and can see and hear the secret, shadowy part in her that is profound, magnificent and necessary.

Taking this concept and exploring it through Ophelia, not only helped me make sense of my own inner darkness but it also helped me make sense of the darkness in others — through story, myths, the lives of other women, archetypes.

Revisiting and channeling through pain, trauma and weakness is not an easy thing to do. Our society has shunned us in many ways from facing our pain, embracing our weaknesses, our darkness and our shadow. We have been trained to think that it is something to avoid, to resist and above all, to hide. We see it as something separate from us. It is because of this kind of thinking that so many of us spend our entire lives never once facing those experiences which have caused us pain, guilt, shame, envy or even those memories which make us believe we are worthless, that we are failures, that we are undeserving of love or friendship or the abundance of our world. It is these feelings that we cast aside, forgetting that without them, we are unable to become an integrated whole. From this understanding, I found the only way to get through Ophelia Wears Black was to create a formula, hidden inside of a poem. The entirety of Ophelia can be found in one poem — a poem I wrote specifically for the sake of remaining focused and deliberate within the nature of my work and the undeniable darkness which has always propelled it. The poem is entitled, *The Black Heart* and it reads:

*"Had I not known all the shades and measures of my own darkness,*
*how else would I have restored my being to this kind of wholeness?*
*Without my darkest sides,*
*I am afraid, I am untrue."*

Through her journey, Ophelia goes back in time to face the experiences in her life which caused her difficulty, grief, added pain and confusion. She allows herself, for the first time, to let her dark travel through her, to make a home of her. She lets it work on her, shows it her palms and lets it read her. She lets it stain her. What she finds is strength in each of her experiences, in all her mourning and grieving, in all her suffering, in all her weakness — a hidden and unique gift: of healing, change, renewal and rebirth. What she finds is perfection in her darkness — perfection in the secret, inner realm that is half her heart, half her face, half her soul.

Ophelia threw me into a wild frenzy of study: from past humans, to psychology, mythology, shadow work, ancient cultures, observations of natural life. I looked to history and basic sciences to sort out the truth and meaning behind these dark phases and the truth of their necessity. I turned to charts illustrating cyclical processes — their beginnings and especially, their dark phases. I sat with all kinds of cycles (plant cycles, moon cycles, human cycles, seasons) and worked hard to find the descending spirals which would assist me in bringing Ophelia's dark quest to life. It was in their closure phases that I found the most interest — in the decay of plant bodies, in the waning moon, in the death of humans bodies and animal bodies. As we all know, every cycle has its end phase — meaning that this "dark side" is an absolute necessity and without it, we are in fact "untrue." I was desperate to write off my formula within *The Black Heart* as truth. I wanted to be sure of it. Observations of the natural world provided me with the courage and conviction to move forward with Ophelia.

Before I looked to cycles, it was shadow work which first affirmed the many points in my so-called "hypothesis." What I found though, was that in order to complete any kind of shadow work, one must be committed to bringing themselves towards the light or, wanting to "shed a light" on that which has been suppressed. For as we all know, it is only in the light a shadow can first be seen. I realized that after spending much time dealing, working and understanding the concepts of the shadow self, what I wanted for Ophelia was blackness — full, rich and complete blackness. I wanted her to lie across the dark side of the moon. I wanted her to descend. I wanted her in the Underworld. I wanted her to come face to face with Eresh-kigal's cold, black tears. I wanted her to follow Persephone down. To lose herself and all of her belongings like Inanna.

I wanted her to "wear her black."

Aside from creating Ophelia's character, it was important to me that the darker elements of the world's two-sided face be expressed in a way that was beautiful, romantic and in a way that confirmed their necessary — a way that challenged the "bad" reputation our darker half has somehow managed to acquire. Our Yin aspect. Femininity. Passivity. The Moon. Shadows. Death. Negativity. Disintegration. The Unconscious. All of these principles which so faithfully have assisted in bringing our magnificent world into being. By resisting the very real truth of this dark side, we resist the truth of who we are and thus, put a dangerous halt on our ability to grow as spiritual beings on the path to expansion. By refusing to face and embrace all of life's cycles and nuances, we deny ourselves of a very crucial part of our existence. There is a part in me, I will admit, one that is very alive, that has written every word in this entire book in an attempt to pay homage to this darker half of the cycle and to obliterate the false and commonly held opinion of it. I have sought here, among other things and as I always have, to show the necessity of this Other side, to lift the veil.

While studying for Ophelia, I found that our culture often exalts only one half our cycle — that of growth and life and because of this, some of us have refused the other half completely. We keep it unseen, we make sure it stays tucked away. We have turned this integral part of our life cycle into something evil, something threatening. The very thought of being in darkness shakes us like a storm and that is because it is in darkness, in the unconscious shadowy realm of the mind, that all of our misfortunes are alive — our shameful longings, our rage, our sorrows, our insecurities, our fears, our trauma, our failures — hidden and sitting like a body of people, a court we do not want to have to see. It is in darkness all of this is kept secret, thrown there in the unconscious. This is why it is feared — because of its power that demands us to face it and be with it, because of its power that demands we work and be challenged by it — the addictions, the mental illness, the abuse and the abuse we have done to others, the ego which is always hungry and never sleeps, the lies we tell ourselves, the lies we believe about ourselves.

When we can find it in us to journey into the depths of our darkness and face it, what we are doing is permitting ourselves to be the recipients of a divine and sacred gift — a gift of healing and regeneration.

It is a necessity to face all that we have lived, head on. We must awaken old monsters, ones which have been asleep due to our negligence and our cowardice, so that we may understand the perfection of those trials and move forward. We must go through the door and do the work that is most difficult. Ophelia is a woman who does this. She does what society says she should not do: she goes back, into past and present darkness and finds the courage to be with it. She knows she will never be strong if she does not revisit those moments in her life which have stifled her. She is with her dead. She is having tea in the misty cavern of her own unconscious. She is waltzing with her shadows, writing poetry with her dark. She is in the Underworld — resolving, transforming, searching for her master key. She is letting her story go — blasting it elsewhere, floating towards the air, conquered in her own history and yet, forever a part of the complete, integrated Ophelia: who is always dying, always living, in the same realm, always at once, and who emerges always, into the new — more powerful than before.

To bring out our dead, to die, to let it all go and consider why it happened and why its important and be proud that it happened— that is purpose of Ophelia Wears Black. As it is only then we can undergo any kind of transformation: we must die and not only must we die but we must be present at our own funeral. We must embrace daily death.

We must "wear our black."

Ophelia Wears Black is divided into four parts: The First Blush, On Solitude & Abandon, Burials and Blood of the Seed. We as humans are seasonal creatures — half of us given to fullness, for giving and growth and our other half, for death, decay, for shedding and rest. The four parts in this book are much the same, mirroring the four cycling seasons of our planet Earth paralleled with stories, myths and experiences that interested me most: innocence, innocence lost, solitude and descent.

The First Blush illustrates the very lonely and yet delicate beginnings endured during childhood's hour. Each of us begin as seed, as sprout, first tender shoot. We are root and stem. We are dependent creatures filled with an intense desire to know, understand and be our own. Each of us begin in the dark and burst forth in being, into greater darkness, into nuances and periods of white light. I have taken Ophelia and sent her on a quest to understand that friendless age. As it is the childhood quest of most in seeking something of Other; in tearing ourselves apart from the world of another and into our own world — in stripping ourselves of our innocence and into knowing. The First Blush is a young, infinitely curious maiden. It is the very force which propels the hand to stroke the flower which leads to the Underworld. It is the profound desire to be seduced by the world beyond. It is the gloomy spring of a woman coming into being, full of promise.

I have found that the human experience is one which undergoes continuous back and forth between states of becoming and unbecoming. On Solitude & Abandon reminds us that the years of early adulthood seem to bring about both: moments of growth, of waxing and thickening and moments of disintegration and ruin. We learn our greatest lessons because we are not exempt from experiencing pain, abandon, annihilation and we do this upon entering this great unknown, this terrifying and magnificent world that awaits us. These challenges we are only capable of conquering in this reality, in this aching form, through suffering and through great difficulty. The more we suffer, the wider the doorway opens; the heavier the animal, the greater the wingspan.

We must come to a place where we begin to love our dangers, our shame and shadow — as they belong to us. Without them, we would be inadequate and unaccomplished. On Solitude & Abandon tells of a few dark themes I felt most appropriate in illustrating the world of adolescence: coming of age, abuse, peer pressure, the awakening of first love, insane hopes and confusions, mistakes, lessons learned. I hope others can revisit their own dark pasts and have the courage to find and identify the perfection of these phases and make peace with them. Honor your suffering, it is your master key. These are the poems of a scalding summer, a burned and black earth.

There are people in this world who die while they are still alive. Burials tells of these people. I learned very early that death does not happen all at once, nor does he appear in one form. Death is a visitor; he hangs around, he haunts. Most of us have seen him, seen his silver eyes which cloud over in their trance, felt the gust of his black wings. Most of us know what it is to die. Burials represents a deepened loneness, the life of a hermit — a time spent in hiding and solitude. It is symbolic of a buried body or perhaps, too, a hibernating bear. The poems here are aimed to express that hiding is an act of self love. Hiding, "dying" to the outside world, is a very private and courageous decision. It is a promise to oneself for reclamation of the spirit and rebirth. To hide, to be away from influence and judgement, is an act of immediate and extreme self love.

We must reject the outer world, for just a little while, to come into communion with an interior, inner-reflective world which is entirely our own, a place where no one can touch us. Hiding, coming face to face with this kind of death, is necessary for our growth. Here, Ophelia vanishes from her own story, into willing abduction — she knows it is sacred practice, a way to protect herself, a way to slow down the mind and create a world of her own. I found it is important to pull inward after great difficulty and renew ourselves, to be away from the world. These are poems of a fall, a soft rest, a vanishing.

The final part of my book, Blood of the Seed, are poems of descent. Descent into the Underworld. Re-imagined from ancient Greek myths, I took Ophelia's character and envisioned her going into her own Underworld where she would have to face the reality of her dark experiences and face them once again. I imagined her going through this great dark unknown and truly being there, in the dark, inviting ruin and understanding it. I imagined her coming to a place where she finds these experiences beautiful. When I began writing, what inspired and propelled me forward was a strong lust to experience and know the material world, now I make it my work to show the journey towards rebirth and transformation is downward — into the underground, into the Underworld, into the dark, inner dimensions of the unconscious.

Only when we have been obliterated can we begin again. Only when we descend, can we ascend. This is the hidden and mysterious promise which resides in the unconscious, in the Underworld, waiting to found by you so that you may burst forth into power and expansion unlocking the magnificence of your own self created Heavens.

This is Ophelia's journey down, through life, trial, the watery realms — through the Earth and into the dark Underworld of her own being.

*For the girl who fell through the Earth*
*and still became Queen;*
*for the winter things.*

# *the*
# BLACK HEART

*"Had I not known all the shades and measures of my own darkness,<br>how else would I have restored my being to this kind of wholeness?<br>Without my darkest sides,<br>I am afraid, I am untrue."*

# *the* FIRST BLUSH

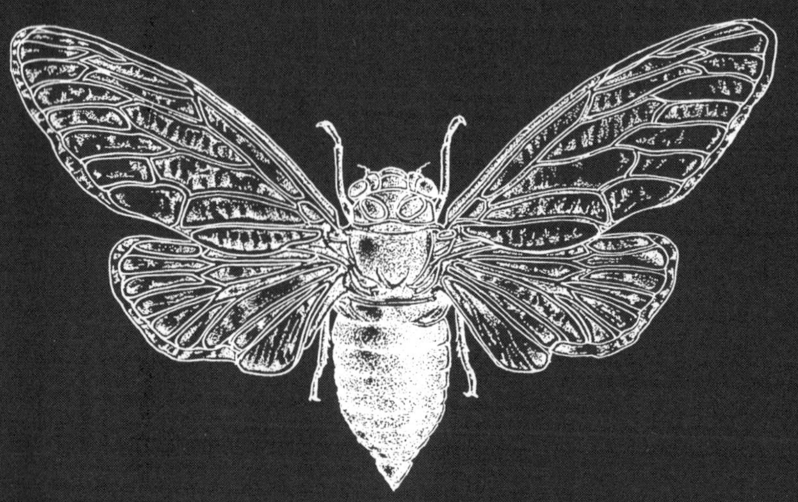

# THE BLACK HAND

*Innocence,*
*which is so often touched by the demon*
*endures a unique kind of suffering…*
*as it is lifted out the lungs of women,*
*thrown from the hearts of men*
*(unseen, yet deeply-felt…)*

*There is no tale about how innocence can*
*survive in the world*

*there is only its undertaking*

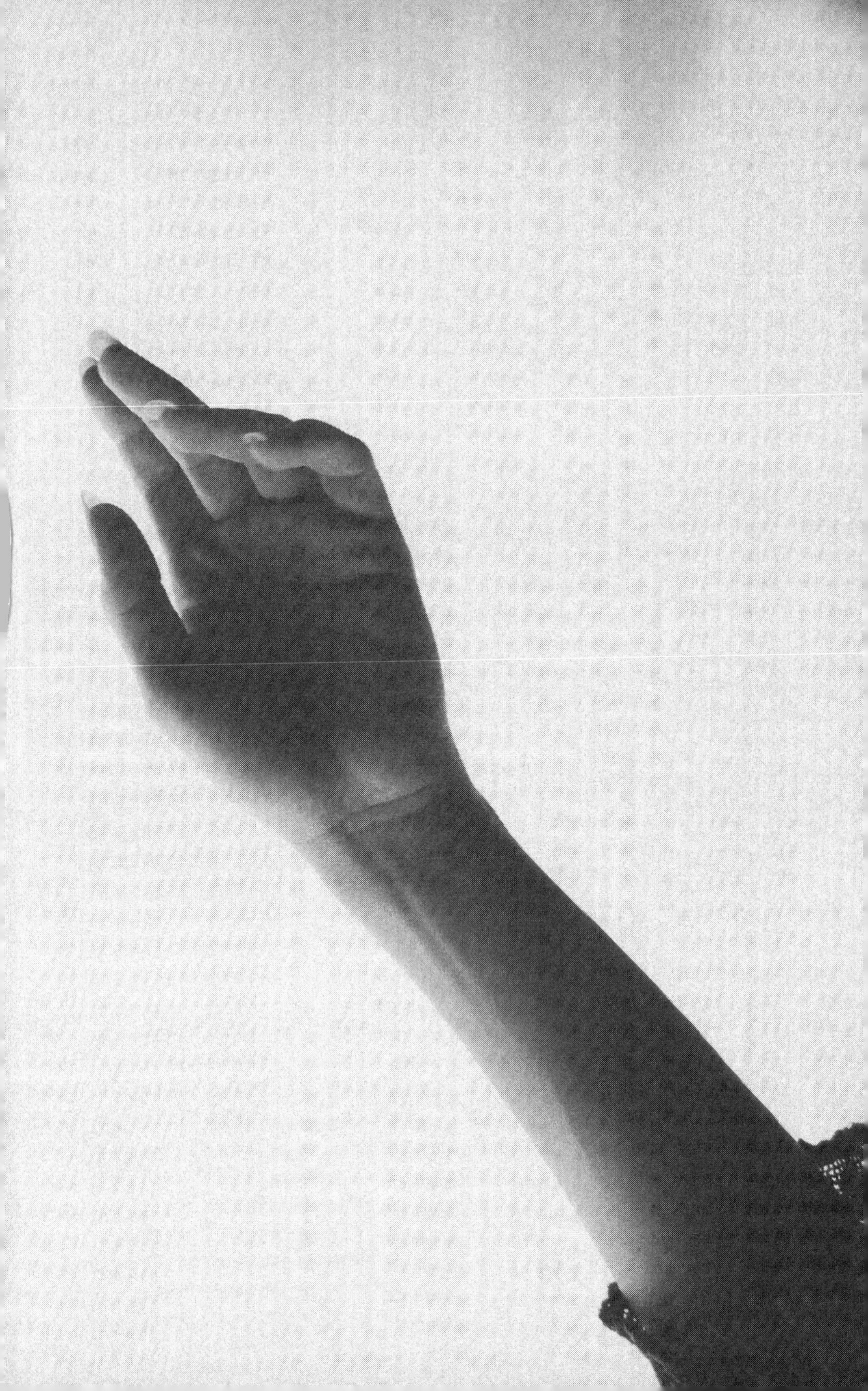

# MOMENTS OF BEING

*It lingers in the mind, those days of childhood*
*where all mystery still seems unexplained...*
*that it is the beginning of all transformations is all I know;*
*the first blush, the opening of the eyes,*
*the wild newness of being so full of presence.*
*We are pushed with gentleness from the undying womb*
*of cosmic space, losing balance between the countless realms of*
*spirit, descending within the walls of the same vessel as the dead*
*which ascend beside us. Into the rawness of earthly manifestation we go:*
*knowing the bitter taste of our strange futures, the taste of our*
*false boundaries, knowing well of our plan, full of suffering and*
*purpose. How we must stay persistent though we are enclosed by*
*unclear depths: the obscure shapes of life's seasons, the*
*formlessness of sound, all these things which precede us; all*
*these things which we know from far away.*

*Alas, we possess and dwell within the empty space of woman,*
*form ourselves into embodiment, nourish our actuality and*
*our absoluteness — we, who become alive in flowing embrace, our*
*human hearts with two chambers beating alongside Earths tremor,*
*drawing out our intended structure, wavering yet fixed — as though*
*it were some kind sorcery, looked to with both wonder and awe,*
*that we may fashion and complete ourselves, make ourselves more*
*human — and in such short time, in the warm, miraculous sea of creation,*
*in the surging abyss; still, we sustain our uniqueness, branching out,*
*reaching, giving way to bolts of celestial grace — binding together the*
*gossamer fabric of genius, interlacing intelligence like the weaving of tales,*
*entwined by what is written, the braid of Genesis. We come, then, to a close; to*
*the first of completions by which all others are now able and within reach*
*for we have created our inmost being, our outwardly existence, the mysterious*
*method of transportation, the moving sanctuary of flesh and blood whereby*
*all tests and truths can now reveal themselves to us. Show yourself, we*
*say. We are sewn together, we are wonderfully made.*

*And with a readiness, we turn over — we withdraw ourselves, abandoning
the cushioned and solemn interior wilderness from which we established
our rarity and we do this by way of rupture, by way of brutal awakening. We are
startled into being — propelled, yet again, from the altar of all that is sacred.
We grow heavy; strangled, for a moment, between two realms, exposed to
sudden sound, movement, the cry of woman; blinded, head first — hanging,
gaining possession of our half-filled bestial frame, hybrid of angel and human.
We come into the world, we come into oblivion, our divine purpose slipping
from the mind for becoming alive was difficult — all at once we are new, trembling,
uninstructed. Yet, even before we are known, we have been loved and so powerful is
our presence as we softly unfold into the newness of our reality; that her heart,
finding evenness and quietness, comes together with exaltation, all of this beside
the rupture and dissolving pain of her human form, she comes together — for us,
the affinity of her soul; at her breast, beside the grace of her heart, we are kept alive.*

*Ah, and what strangeness is our infancy! Every moment, terrifying: the very
act of seeing — a surging mass of deep feeling, information of all previous
lives with their vague remembrance floating towards the air. O movement, o sound,
o unveiling radiance, yes; you have shown yourself, all is filled with you. We
are tired but we will hold on. We are here now in the ceaseless message, in the
realm of the unkind, in the current of life which may hinder our soul from
moving onward. We are here now. All this is mission and though we are consumed
with the sobbing of our dark spring, helpless and dependent other creatures,
still, we are graced by the flowering sweetness of one voice and the tide of winter
begins to thaw: we endure our vulnerability to then outgrow it suddenly, to be freed of
it like snake skin and as if done overnight, so quickly do we grow from our
defenselessness — where we were once blind and disadvantaged now we are
quick and able, filled with the intense desire to know, to understand the indefinite
world which is brimming with color, crowded with the thunderous roar of both the
living and the dead, overflowing with adventure and static — begging to be touched,
tampered with by our own infinitely eager hand. We are displaced by the
outside world, overthrown by first longings, lured in by the here and now, by our
eagerness to march into the unknown, to take our boat and sail uncharted waters.*

# FIRST BORN

*We come into existence, we are born —*
*some say we are born innocent and clean...*
*but I know that that which is born,*
*is first born wild, barbaric —*
*is born shaking and without law,*
*is born hungry.*

# THE EYES OF A CRONE

*There is nothing in me that could prevent life from entering,*
*life sharpens itself agaisnt me, the greatness of a day leaves no gap,*
*the stuff of girls belongs to yesterday. I ask for it now, I beckon*
*that it come upon me, almost fatally, violently, now — waste me away.*

*Come now, my door is unlocked — I will hang loosely, like a petal,*
*like a slanting hand, before the salivating mouth of a life below.*

*My friend is the clock — and I have loved behind its walls, a thing of the past,*
*collecting pasts, hoarding stories, imagining myself as life's young bride —*
*I put on my mother's dress and the dress kept her shape.*

*I, who am not my own, fear I will die before I have known dark secrets, evils,*
*before they are given the chance to shape my heart. Frighten me, disfigure my heart,*
*I will die before I have been drunk with life and love and known the dark groans of Hell!*

*At night I dream and am astounded.*

*I see men, I see women — kissing, stretching the bone, tearing the quietude*
*with laughter and tear; their faces, moving seas — for seas are dancing things.*
*Roar and whisper. Body and shore. Coat of fur and coat of cloud.*
*Ancient blue monster of drifting ash, cold, unknowable mist.*

*It is in dreams, I know the fever of love and am loved by many.*
*It is in dreams, I have friends — creatures, whose beards shoot forth, bristling like dry earth and I am glad when they are near me, I am less alone. They sleep in my hair and convince me of strange things, and from my heart, blood wells and falls, to know lies from friends — cuts, aren't they? Slits in the murmuring heart?*

*I only see them in the night.*

*I see beauty and terror — no one tells you they are one in the same...*
*that kind of secret is the stuff of dreams. They ache as we ache*
*for they are living things, breathing things, each turns the blood —*
*fast and sharp, never to return as they once were.*

*Beauty to fire. Terror to ice. The blood knows these things.*

*I see jewels which glow with drowsy, easy pleasure — flirting, batting eyes.*
*I lie in gardens of serpents and cannot tell what is my hair or which are my limbs.*
*We make our love. We lie in the grass like wounded things.*

*Impossibilities.*

*I want to grow heavy with pain and then find it in me to unburden myself with*
*unspeakable joys. I want to know the face of God. I want to see his teeth.*
*I want to know what makes him hungry and if he'd weep the day life goes out,*
*the same way I weep now for my life, this non-life, this life of dreams?*
*I want to know the hand of the Devil, to hold it, close as a ghost, a hand dressed*
*in blood — and if there is moving blood in him at all, is it thick or thin?*
*Red or black? Of fire or ice?*

*What did they call him before he lived?*
*What shall they call me once I have lived?*

*A demon girl with horn and wing? A woman shaped shadow?*

*I want to know. I want to pull back the skin. I say:*
*I want life to fall from me. I want to be a weeping and red sky;*
*tears which fall from the eyes of a Crone.*

# HUNTING DRESS

*You who dress and feed me, dress me now for I am your doll;*
*curl my raven hair, powder my rear and tie my black bow.*
*I will wait at the corner, if you ask. I will do anything you ask.*
*I will be silent and still, like water in a glass, like unhurried clouds.*

*I will be silent and still, just like you ask.*

*I will stand and wait for you, looking out, into the teeming world:*
*up at the albatross, down at the worm, across at the fields, around —*
*at the breezes filled with imperfect things: blood, prayer, breath, curses.*
*I will wait for you and behold the dead and my joy will be like no other.*

*Silent and still. You take my brother from his lock.*

*This morning, beneath my coat, you must have placed a hunting dress…*
*like a huntress, I am silent and still, eyes peering out, one at a time.*
*I will wait at the corner, just like you asked, I will wait behind the tall grass*
*until the time is right, until the sun goes down, until all of life nestles down.*

*This body is a ticking clock.*

# WINTERESS

*That which is wild moves to its own law,*
*always changing, always hot, cheating death.*
*I learned early I was a cold girl — nothing more,*
*unyielding, fixed — unreachable, unchangeable.*
*A being like me, wilts in the sun —*
*leave me in my winter,*
*here I am powerful.*

# KORE

*What, then, does it mean to be good, to be young and innocent?*
*I have come into existence good and innocent and been suppressed.*
*I have simply come into existence, young and innocent and done*
*nothing for it, no work, no great difficulty. I have assumed this reality,*
*virginal and without sin. I have done nothing to be good and yet,*
*you say I am good. You say I am pure because I am untouched by life.*
*To be untouched by life, is to be untouched by light. Is that which is*
*good and young, then, in full darkness? For now, I am unconscious,*
*I am dead and without life. I am buried, stifled, I am the deep core of darkness.*

*I am standing in my dark robe before the treasures of life and I fear*
*it is the strings of sorrow which hold me, to and fro, I swing like a doll*
*before the gates of being, never once to graze the knob, never once to*
*open the door. You say you do not understand my sorrows, how can it*
*exist inside a body which has neither lost nor grieved? You say it is an unknown,*
*unwarranted sorrow for my life is good and filled with love. But I have*
*grieved and o, I am losing now — for my life, to me, is not even a shadow —*
*for even shadow can only be seen amidst the break of day, amidst a sun*
*which casts its dark body out to mingle with the unobscured. I say, I am in*
*blackness, full blackness. I am in blackness — full, rich blackness.*

# CHILD OF DREAMS

*Child of dreams —*
*born in the deep freeze of February,*
*wandering, moving through the land,*
*playing God with her mind of savage wonder;*
*her bones made of heartsease, her flesh of blue,*
*friends with both faerie and beast*

*brought forth from the womb, middle-aged,*
*she, who could see all things, knew she had been here before*
*beside her private clouds, the slow breathing wilderness,*
*the flickering sensation of time...*
*speaking with the birds and breathing beneath the sea,*
*unafraid of the harm that may await*

# THE OTHER

*To look in the mirror and witness ones smallness,*
*the limbs which have not yet come their conclusions —*
*unaware of how they will warp and curve into their own originality;*
*always, to look into the mirror and feel so much more*
*than ones own humanness — especially as a child,*
*whose body soars beyond the bounds, a second body.*
*Feeding, speaking in fabricated dialogues to all creatures,*
*both of the world and of their own mind, to spirits both with and without form*
*and especially to thine own self, rustling secrets before the glass.*

*To look in the mirror and recognize such smallness....*
*when in all children, exists such future, such inward pull —*
*kept in the body where all imagination streams,*
*all becomes life, twists into world, journeys out with able wings,*
*through the water, with gill and fin and scale.*
*All this inside, entombed, the deep pull of Other.*

*O, to know it — to come to this knowing,*
*that the body must not be all there is, that it must only grow*
*to then exhaust itself and inside have gathered all the gifts*
*of spirit, of knowing, of imagination,*
*all, within the small hour by which our lives are lived,*
*that one hour, perhaps a day, by which this one life is lived.*

# DAUGHTER

*Upon being born, I was pressed suddenly upon the breast of a saint,*
*suddenly — upon her heart, blared the horn of weeping angels,*
*their opera of stolen innocence. It echoed in the recesses of my heart,*
*it blew through me with vigor and grief, it — dug a hole, like an animal,*
*in the lair of my newfound being. It quickened my breath, my heart —*
*actualized it from that dark, wax-like matter and taught me*
*the inner workings of a woman's private suffering.*

*I was born the daughter of both Atheist and Saint.*
*I came into the world divided, as though both Life and Death*
*fought, during the hours of my birth, for the right of my humanly existence.*
*Their war has its dominion over my face —*
*my eyes, the beating black wings of Death,*
*my face, the pale reflection pond of Life.*

*I was born out the womb of the most innocent, by the impulse of evil.*
*The shadows of my body tell the tale of a love which should not have been,*
*but still, became — by rapture of promised escape, by defiance of one's own fate.*
*My neck of ivory, my mouth of smoke — all this which seeks to define me,*
*all this deep feeling which declares war in me — all of this...*
*which drowns my voice in its thunderous roar.*

*I am split with great mystery.*

*I am both living and dead,*
*haunted upon the sea of the heart.*

# SPRINGTIDE

*Springtide,*
*you have your rule,*
*your rough beginnings which defy all doubt —*
*you open up before the world, emitting your essence…*
*You, who follow the winter, passage out — unafraid,*
*overflowing, disobedient, flowering into creation*
*with task, with vigor. It would seem nothing now,*
*nothing is so influential as your defiance,*
*your rebellion and your quivering flourish.*

*I have witnessed your work, the author of my own form,*
*my slow birth. Often I gaze at this form in wonder,*
*stand at the edge of my own equinox, recall it to mind.*
*There is the bud, so at home, beauty and strangeness.*
*O, had this been a gentler world perhaps I wouldn't think*
*of this frame as such — such risk you drew out in me,*
*such danger you pulled from me, to make me woman was*
*an act of sacrifice, wasn't it? The round breasts which*
*rose from nothingness — the wide hip, the full lip which*
*taunts blindly with desire. So often now, I have tried to*
*undo your work: make a mute of myself, keep secret the*
*nature of my character. Yet still, all of you arises within*
*me to mean beginning: darkly and in order.*

# FEBRUARY

*The first breaths I took as I entered this World were that of Winter:*
*cold and unforgiving, full of death and rebirth. It is the month of*
*February which carries the remains, the debris, the decay —*
*and passes them into spring (into its laughing mouth).*

*The bones of a year since passed fall upon February —*
*collector of ash and dust. Death mother. Winter crone.*
*Often time, I look at myself in the mirror and the frost of February*
*fills me like fragrance, a tinge — once white, now many hued,*
*merely degrees of darkness and darkness, vast death;*
*once unseeable, now seen and begs of me to be old while I am young.*

*My dark inscription:*
*death before me, beneath me, behind all things.*
*Gilded, ore; darkening as a sea darkens.*

*Being dead — does the same,*
*fills me with a silence greater than a god's mouth.*

*Till March comes*
*to suck the poison out...*

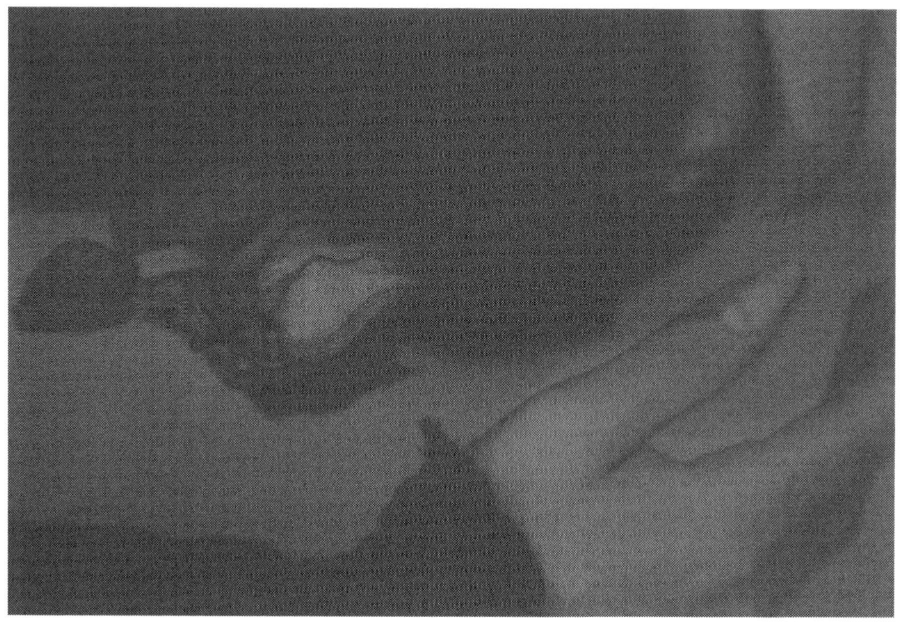

# GIRLHOOD

*Out of solitude, my childhood yearns, a twisted vine —*
*with its unusual state of loneness and helplessness,*
*when everything nestles down (slow, slow down…)*
*the longing for girlhood emerges, like a flower which unfurls*

*and without regard, the yearning for its original*
*condition: pure, innocent — infinitely tender screams*

*I am pressing towards what was once unstained, more true —*
*the small animal of my body, the creature which remains*
*in my womb holds to the memory of girlhood like a slave*

# THE GIRL
# &
# THE WOMAN

*The state between the girl and the woman*
*is not a delicate blossoming,*
*but an unraveling,*
*a suffering,*
*a humiliating transformation*
*I, myself, have never been the butterfly,*
*but the overgrown, undone cocoon*
*half-winged, half-loved and half alive*
*eternally suspended between realities*

# IN THE HOLLOW OF A HAND

*I walked enchanted, playing dreamer,*
*wishing myself small, secretive and silent.*
*Fitting, like a grain, in the hollow of a hand...*
*away from all danger, away from wild jungles —*
*from their obstacles where all is married, mating,*
*creeping across, thrown and twisted, nameless.*
*Where all is shown who is king.*

*I wanted no king.*

*I'd think myself up in the heart of a fist, a fist-like cave —*
*sleeping, loving, wandering through the mind as small and*
*unseen as a mouse;*

*wandering through*

*a cold, blue fist — his skeleton's claw.*

# BODY OF DARKNESS

*What body is not first nursed in darkness,*
*what corpse does not then lay in soft dark,*
*what soul does not first drag itself through black clouds*
*to then know again the unpoliced break of day?*

*I had come to darkness*
*and found I had come to my own.*

# THE FACE

*Had my heart a face,*
*it would be that of a child's —*
            *cheeks turned towards Heaven,*
*tears streaming towards Hell*

# WRAITH

*Before my life began, I was convinced I would grow to be a woman who would die young. I didn't know how or when, I only knew it by invisible hunch. I knew what I would go through yet I could not see my life unfold passed a certain age. I felt my body growing alongside a kind of death but still — how is it that as a child, knowing no death, no loss, could have brought herself forth to such predetermination? How does one, enveloped in the veil of innocence, place themselves by the open doorway of the house of God? How is it that I kept this inside of me, as though death itself hollowed out my frame and made me unafraid, full of rebellion with a dangerous need for solitude? How did I, who was made of youth and innocence, contain the whole of death so willingly? I know now that what emerged from me then was not future... but rather, an innate ability to let go of all things and to drift, towards stillness, to see the other side, to fall into it without question or resistance —*

*like the loosening of a cocoon from its mantle, filled beyond fulfillment, by such long and everlasting fall; an afterlife.*

## MOTHER'S MILK

*How painful it is to exist in a world where one does not belong…*
*how painful to suffer ones rarity alone, with no one to fall akin —*
*holding ones body steady in the wind;*
*where shadows meet and swing pass the flowing air —*
*till dawn brings rescue, I am in darkness.*

*It spills from my open mouth, it is my mother's milk —*
*it both nourishes and destroys, thickens and softens,*
*it — quiets my blood and makes me strong:*
*my weapon takes all forms — in darkness: I exist —*
*I grow old, I mature, I stare with all eyes, beyond —*
*with a gaze that breathes.*

# BLACK SUNS

*To be innocent and kind, that is the work of angels, as well as ecstasy — tremendous intensities: pain, pleasure, hypnosis. Are these not, too, the work of angels? I used to believe in divisions. I used to believe in good and evil. I used to believe in Heavens and Hells. Now I believe in everything. All of it as one vast, provoking spiral of ascent and descent. As a girl, I dreamt of black suns. I dreamt of the seven gates of the Underworld. I dreamt of passaging through them, of being strangled by Persephone's dark wet air, of my soles bruised with blue from her teary-eyed caverns. It was not Hell itself I feared, what I feared most what not experiencing it for myself. What I feared was that it would remain unknown to me — that I would die, and never once taste dark water or eat of forbidden fruit. I was innocent and kind — and yet, endured the most violent upsets so incredibly because of my hunger for life and before that, because of my preoccupation with death. When life came for me, I drank from her cup — without expectation, without suspicion. I swam aggressively in the Atlantic, kicking my feet, turned up — towards the sun, beads of sea and salt across my brow. The sun would kiss me and it always hurt. And when death came for me, it took on many forms: night, solitude, grief. Periods of solitude, nights still and without life, deep within, I took pleasure in the physical pain of a momentary death, suffused with its own goodbyes. I endured the joy and pain which came from the daily discovery of "opposites." The work of angels, it seems, knows no segregation, neither split nor crack. I have found beautiful surprise and transformation, found life within my yearning for death and death within my need for life. I have found union with that which everyone had once convinced me was separate and disunited.*

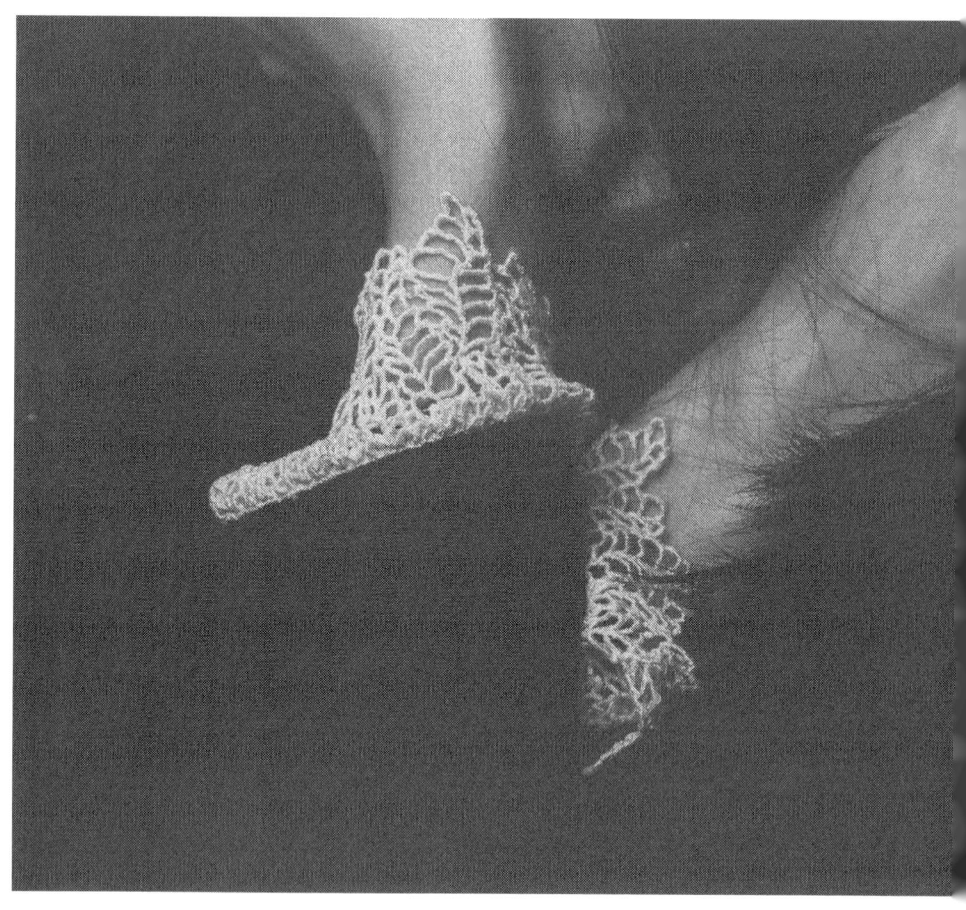

# THE WHISPER

*Something whispered.*
*I reached my hand to it…*
*as it seemed nothing was alive there, but a chill,*
*an unforgettable nothingness.*
*Yet I suspended my disbelief.*
*I offered my body to the unknown, to fear,*
*to the mysterious blindness —*
*and it was then, and only then,*
*I found magic*
*moving in the underground*

# MOON MAIDEN

*Moon maiden,*
*I understand it now,*
*how, silently, you gave yourself to the night*
*abandoning all duty, stepping into worlds more graceful than your own*
*through your books, full of romance, Queens and Kings,*
*castles made of air, knights, women of unrivaled beauty....*
*you were able to live the life you had dreamed of as a girl*
*and so, secretly, you let them possess you*
*silently, as they awoke your imagination, as they unfurled,*
*you rose to greet them like a woman coming of age, like an autumn breeze*
*made love to them, mothered them, suspended time...*

*You surrendered to them... walked out into invisible worlds —*
*in your gown of white, sewn by seated angels, paler than bone*
*your hair, blacker than obsidian, which protected you through and through,*
*you let the workings of your soul take you where you wished to be*
*and only for a moment, a second of your lifetime*
*for as long as it would have you — for you would always return,*
*with a swiftness, to the monochromatic world*
*you had been cast to*

*I understand it now:*
*the longing in your eyes for your secret worlds,*
*even when you held me there was the gaze of Other, of distant lands,*
*there were deep silences, there was the devotion to your*
*shelves of paperback, their secret worlds...*
*I understand it now — the longing to escape,*
*the craving, the desire which adorns the heart.*
*O, but how you always returned and this, you did for me*
*because with your entirety, you loved me*

*O, I say now:*
*that is love, that is love! — to stay, to return*
*even when all of one desires to leave*

# DAWN OF LOVE

*Even when it became familiar to me, there was this:*
*the dawn of love — the first kiss like the cascade of angels,*
*like smoke ascending from ancient lands, unveiling rapture.*
*There was always this: the foundation from which it first unfolded*
*like the opening of palms, fingers spreading apart —*
*a testimony to their own revolution, to have in one's hand another.*

*There is nothing like one's first,*
*the intensity of ones own violent heartbeat,*
*the hymn which is not of the world but of the elementals —*
*where fire meets earth, flames which*
*occupy the bodies of two human creatures…*
*the serpent of love dances within them both,*
*uniting them by the mouth and suddenly, bursting,*
*explosive aches of affection, the tenderness: a blooming cut*

# LAMB

*You say I am your lamb.*

*You enclose me in your arms and pet me behind the neck,*
*oh, soft, little lamb — a stroke, beautiful black lamb…*
*and a kiss to seal your truth: that I am your quiet, simple lamb.*

*Your thoughts of me, they pass from you like dreams,*
*you forget them like memories of your own childhood, like old letters.*
*You, who would watch as shadows pass through me.*
*You, who would have me under heaven's gaze if you could.*

*You work your old hands into my soft black curl, claiming it your own.*
*I close my eyes and feel like no lamb.*

*In me, I feel a great capacity for unspeakable harm and while*
*I am at your teat, muzzled in your breast, it is a ghost in air, in shroud*
*that I follow with my own wandering gaze. You ask me what I look at,*
*you laugh, unaware — and if I could speak I'd tell you:*

*death is near, cloaking us, always whispering*

*and you'd think me no lamb.*

# MOUTHFUL OF SORROW

*When I was a child, they called me a little girl and when I grew,*
*they called me a young woman. How strange a thought —*
*when I've always felt more like a pit of fire, a black sea of passion,*
*a mouthful of sorrow, a league of fallen angels.*

# BLACK HORSE

*There is a black horse outside that waits for me.*
*You will not stop me. If you pull me by the arms as I leave your house,*
*if you draw your sword, if there is struggle upon my departure,*
*it is another body you will retain, it is another skin you will throw*
*upon your lawn. It will not be me, for I am already gone.*

*I have mounted his muscular frame, I have wrapped my pale arms*
*around his body. Yes, I already love him and I will follow him down.*

*on*

# SOLITUDE & ABANDON

# HYDRA

*It was love that broke open my heart,*
*gave it unusual form*
*and filled it with strange ways*

# THE DWELLING

*Now I will be my own — what form will I take?*
*It is in darkness I have dwelled and have been hungry like a grave.*
*Death hangs around. I look him in the face: a task beyond all strength,*
*to take him in like scent and, as in a dream, continue through, darkly and*
*side by side, hand-in-hand, onward — escaping, like lovers, some old life.*
*I take him in and hold my breath till I am blue, till it hurts,*
*till the heart stops — bring me home, bring me home.*

*I am wearing the bones of my innocence, a crown of shooting bone.*
*Deep within me, I once was a child and died as children die, peering*
*into the eyes of strange faces, bodies of blood, their groins of ecstasy,*
*their mouths full with unknowns.*

*I have put myself on the wave of rapturous bliss.*
*I have put myself in harms way.*
*I have grazed the flower they say leads to another world.*

*I am waiting for the Earth:*

*to hawk, to bark, to rupture —*
*to open its mouth and salivate, to spirit me away,*
*into its dark clustered room, into its deep dark jail.*

# TINGE

*Love begins, a tinge — a dash, then, as if by night: consumes,*
*washes up the hands — fills up each mouth, arrests the heart,*
*entangles the mind, the blood — till all is devoured by love.*
*I am afraid I had not learned this before you: to stand there nakedly,*
*amidst danger. For nothing vast had entered me, not like this — this*
*deliverance of a once simple self. For love, I have placed my*
*heart on the grounds of everlasting fire. I have watched it burn*
*and I have been made glad because of it. I will let love damage*
*me raw with ruthless magnificence. I have been ignited by love.*
*It is love to whom I owe my life. I, who am indescribably innocent,*
*am now very much alive in love. I have tasted now the strange fruit*
*of togetherness, my once solitary hands now caught within the black*
*hair of a girl. At rest, I am in love — not just in love, but — vanished*
*within love, possessed by love. Is not everything more vibrant now?*
*Is not everything mad and immortal, divine? I have known no greater*
*force. I am afraid I knew nothing until the moment our mouths came*
*together like the seconds — such rapture, such joy — no matter the*
*distance. Love, to me, is as raw as a wound and yet, it is a door.*
*Now I have peered in. Now it is I whose hands know weight, blood*
*which ebbs and flows, longing. Now it is I, once but a disintegrating*
*shade, now — overrun by fire, orbiting among the stars.*

# INNOCENCE LOST

*Before you,*
*there I was — foolishly mothering innocence*
*like an attendant, peeling over the workings of time —*
*halting it, pulling it apart; fueling the stillness of*
*my own untried space*

*and then you came…giving value to my existence,*
*outdoing, surpassing the Material World*

# MAKE THE LASH DARK

*I have my wounds and so great is their resemblance to your own*
*that it frightens me to look upon your face most days, it is like looking into*
*a mirror or witnessing the bust of god enter a weakening body,*
*a mind drifting away — like something which should remain unseen yet, it*
*is shown and it annihilates me, throws me from my solitude.*

*I want to love those things in you which are dark and improper, full of*
*sorrow and rage. I want to love them as only I can love them, as they have*
*never been loved before — not because they belong to you, but because they*
*are my own throes of rage, my own hours of sorrow and by loving you, I*
*will find it in me to love and walk, in the night, with my own dark.*

*In our darkened time of loving, you have spoken and it is my own voice*
*I hear. You have confessed and it is my own confessions I hear. You weep*
*and it is my own salt I taste upon my mouth. O, you fall to sleep and it is my*
*own world which fades and recedes from me. You go —*
*into the dark and it is not alone that you go.*

# BLUE HYDRANGEA

*How terrifying — and yet how*
*exhilarating it is to know that*
*there are cries in me which*
*are still unheard*

# TRUE BEAUTY

*True beauty*
*is not of the body or of the face,*
*no, it is a thing of the soul —*
*of fire and air, breath and spirit,*
*something brave and unafraid.*

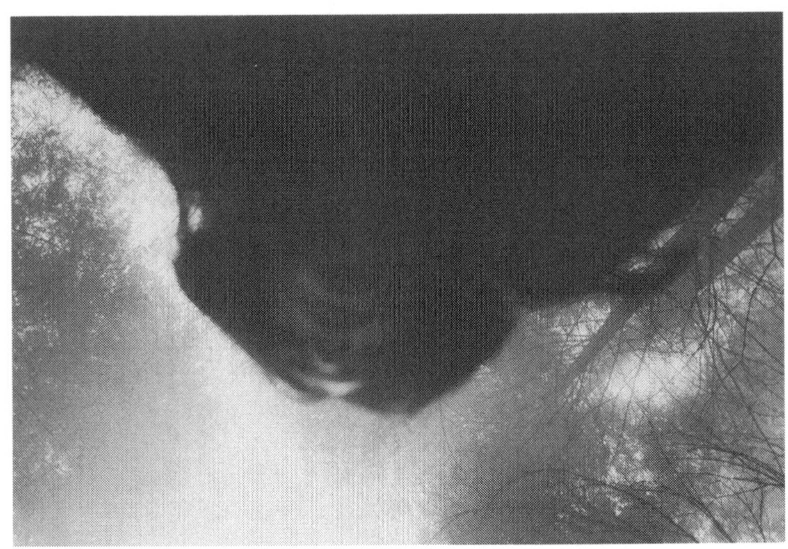

# THE WOUND

*Each time I love (no matter who or what it is)*
*fiercely, readily,*
*it is a wound I open —*
*like a hole*
*dug by the animal in me:*
*I let that which I love*
*crawl inside*

# YEAR OF THE TIGER

## I

*From love, we slipped into midnight like the death of the sun*
*we ran through empty streets, our limbs twisting like white flags of surrender,*
*the ground swelled with the poems of our body and our soles*
*deepened into the Earth, fracturing the dust like the breaking of hearts...*
*for the first time, we held hands, laced them together like vines,*
*exhausting our innocence, hurling it into the darkness,*
*we watched it grow wings and laughed as it grew dim like the moon*

*You said, "I am afraid of loving you, I know it will consume me."*
*yet we kissed beneath trees, enclosed in their bark, shedding their leaves*
*gasping for breath, pale flesh upon flesh, weighty billows of*
*passion seeped from our mouths, our tongues of eloquence and cruelty—*
*like the mingling of dead poets. We were terrified of our own hearts,*
*drawing up wounds, wilted by one another like the wrinkles and*
*delicate folds of an antique wedding dress*

*O, the places you took me... we danced on the darker side of twilight, you and I....*
*found solace in the clatter of bottles, unburdened our bodies with the*
*rhymes of women before us. O, we knew too much, we knew too much and*
*what a violence it was to know and feel so much and yet what a birthright—*
*to feel all the cries of the world, the mourning of the cosmos, the dark*
*weeping of the heavens...rooted and multiplied beneath our mortal, faultless*
*flesh and so we welcomed our wildness...because our bodies were too small, too*
*young to contain the all-embracing stream of life that flowed from them*

*but yet, we couldn't contain one another...*

*We only kissed till our jaws seemed bruised with savagery, silent beside each other,*
*we let resistance grow, sat aware of the hour and tortured one another with the*
*secret language of our femininity. We lit cigarettes together for the first time,*
*blew the dangerous smoke into the spaces we breathed, watched as they*
*came together, retreated from one another and finally, consumed one another*
*like the union of lost love. We were devoted to their dance, how freely they moved —*
*those queens of air, we envied them — how they could at once come into existence,*
*lunging forward from our pained bodies and twist themselves before us with such*
*exquisiteness...then with a swiftness, know all the secrets of disappearance.*

*How we wished to know them too...to know of vanishing — the unrevealed,*
*impossibility of vanishing. Perhaps even if it meant throwing ourselves off*
*dangerous heights, imagining our bodies suspended in time, our black hair*
*waving behind us like mangled black wings. We yearned to disappear most days*
*but instead, given our limitation, we sat and watched the smoke make the*
*kind of love we feared to...and instead of throwing our small frames from*
*cliffs, we poured our heaviness into poetry and drank in our despair.*

*And it went on like that for a few years...*
*two recluses who did all the things we weren't supposed to, knew all*
*the things young girls shouldn't know, searching for ways to*
*cease the insatiable hunger of our countless dreamworlds,*
*desiring the world, loving each other and wanting to die*

*until we grew wings,*
*until our soles knew of freedom*

## II

*The women I walked with walked with chaos*
*they looked to be loved, idolized, remembered...*
*we wore halos of smoke and sought to make dying beautiful.*
*We, who were once greener than Eden, free of sin and bursting*
*with the blush of paradise, by night became a band of wild gypsies,*
*dark haired women who believed we were men inside...*
*we loved like men, fought and fucked like men, drank like men —*
*that was us... underaged, deathless — chafing away...*
*desperate to throw away our delicate youth...*
*so that we could write of something other than*
*our fragile girlish hearts. We draped our hearts in gowns of black*
*and went out — wilder than midnight. We removed from our*
*shoulders the wings of our youthfulness and replaced them*
*with the dark wings of rebellion, with savage bolts of war.*

*We kept our hair short, fashioned ourselves both male and female,*
*anything, anything to cut ourselves out from our physical bodies —*
*which were bruised with the fusion of our pain*
*anything, anything to shock, to dismantle the people from their nests*
*I, with my childish thirst, would have followed them anywhere —*
*to the ends of the underworld, on a boat across, towards the abyss.*

*With them, I believed my heart was made of stone....*
*I believed I could be in my own heart alone — that I was*
*ever capable of concealing my tenderness and my ache*

*There was an untamable beauty about them,*
*they didn't deny the wild which ran through their blood.*

*Birthed from the sea,*
*these women had salt in their wounds —*
*there was poise in their snarl,*
*their faces like that of women whom have lived,*
*their cheeks adorned with permanent salt —*
*dark Aphrodites of revolt and disorder, their bouquets of smoke —*
*could make a man fall to his knees, their war cry I adopted as my own*

*Yes, they were wild, like budding roses*
*beside the scars of our past,*
*that is how I'd like to remember them...*
*in the company of flowers,*
*devouring the violets*

# DUST

*We were in the air once, you and I — weakening into the dust,*
*carried, into the ash of those who loved this fiercely before us,*
*slipping, tumbling into the breeze. We lost our balance, my love —*
*too quickly, we took in the remains of lost love by the mouth. Asphyxiated.*
*I am afraid we taught ourselves how to lose love, to force death upon it.*
*We played God with our love until it was still and without life.*
*It was us, it was always us — who held our love by the throat,*
*beneath dark water, until it shook like a small beast, until it poured*
*forth, casted out before us, before our hands, covered in black.*

*Did you ever know it was you who awakened my heart, it was you*
*who lifted the veil and brought me forth, into life? It was you who*
*led me to lower worlds. It was you who governed the hour of my fall,*
*the hour by which my innocence scattered into dust before us and flew,*
*into awful winds. How can anyone explain what happened between us?*
*The magnitude of our private revivals. I suppose you do not know. How*
*could you know? You belonged to the world and I, to the road before me*
*with a body made of glass. It is you who has shown me I am made of glass.*

*It is I who will spend all of my days, wandering in this limbo, trying*
*to make sense of this pendulous, blood-streaked thread which hangs from*
*my heart like the evidence of time, this thread which has been cut from me*
*by your hand, this damned thread which swings before me like a body of suicide*

*and pounds through me like a league of angels who say I have been fooled,*
*who say I have been taken from, that I have been harmed —*
*by that which I have loved before all else.*

# END OF INNOCENCE

*Once I filled my hands with you.*
*Your dark blood turned beneath my palms*
*and changed my own blood.*

# THE BEAST

*It is God who knows for whom I tremble.*
*Yes, it has always been God whose eyes have known my wanting,*
*my shamefulness, my pity, my ugly — my serpentine hiss, my rattling need.*
*All of this which I desire in secret.*

*It is God who has seen me, naked as a babe. It is he, she, it, beast, bird —*
*who has seen my dark love (who has known you, too) for it is in my heart*
*that you grow, a small beast, and this God has seen my heart with his*
*many wandering eyes, his forces focused inward — his ancient, bruised eye.*

*It is Heaven that knows I love you in unspeakable ways*
*and Heaven it is alone — not even a breeze, not even the night.*

*My love for you climbs walls, it seems…it has limbs and feet, muscle and claw.*
*It does not rest. Breathlessly, it begs; it is untamed. It does not know there is*
*an impossible between us. It does not know your spider's web. Willingly,*
*it enters, with its exhausted body, into your labyrinth, your fine lacework.*

*and it is glad to be near you, the object of my pain and poetry,*
*my slow and rising passion.*

# ANJA

*Shall I show you now how I have cherished you?*
*Beside all known deception, still, I have brought forth*
*my frail, naked body, this very solid hallucination —*
*now, towards your mirror, where you step out to meet me*
*and touch me and give me your command:*

*a death to that name, a star in her place.*

*Once, I grew and was given to roundness. I was swollen*
*with childhood — full as a cry, red as a rabbit's eye...*
*I moved, curious as a shadow, and life spun from me like*
*thread and now I have no memory of such a feeling for that*
*was my old life and all it does is loom like a ghost, never speaking,*
*growing hot behind me, sighing into the string of my hair.*

*I wonder where it is you poured the spell*
*(in, by the throat or through, to the eyes?)*
*so skillfully, you imitated the sky with its weightlessness —*
*you made me believe in false heavens*

*I have watched myself go to you. I have followed you, seen you*
*and known you without other desire. But how often I have*
*arrived at myself, troubled and dismayed, shown a glimpse*
*of my once recognizable form...looked into the mirror where*
*my own eyes deceive me — what terrible sight, what sorrow.*

*Misery sings: a light has gone out.*

*Where is it that I may exist without you?*
*I have blinked a thousand times and still, you exist and only*
*you exist — holding me, at your breast, we sway like two black*
*peaks agaisnt the wintered air and into your bed, I climb, I glide,*
*a winter thing...with no blood to be moved, no beating heart, contained:*
*in the night, in the black, where no one can find me.*

*O, Anja, I am small — the two of us will walk out together*
*and you will fall into my eyes and empty at last,*

*I will die in chains —*
*your snow on my wings.*

# DEVIL'S DAUGHTER

*There are days*
*my pain is so elaborate...*
*that the salt of my tears tastes not of my own...*
*but like that of my ancestors —*
*and the women who dealt with this sorrow*
*before me*

# PHANTOM

*Your heart must be a ghost.*
*I can feel it mounting; a dark wave —*
*upon the night of my soul.*

# EXTINGUISH ME

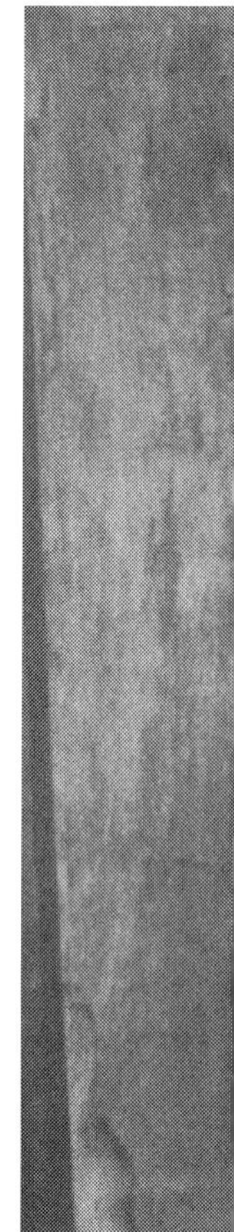

*As a girl, I wasn't drawn to romances.*
*I longed for a quiet, solitary life freed from it...*
*but like all young girls, romance came uninvited and demanding.*
*When it came, it was uncommon, yet deeply rooted...*
*as though I was condemned to, sentenced to it —*
*like a flower which lives its small life in human homes,*
*leaning — with its unnatural bends,*
*towards the s u n*

*I have, like most women,*
*let romance make a victim of me...*
*with a working, conscious heart,*
*I let it extinguish me*

# DAHLIA

*You have a beautiful mind, she said.*
*Its hollows and grooves remind me of a*
*black dahlia, its roundness like caverns*
*of the Underworld...it springs forward*
*like an orchid, lures me in like quicksand*
*and at times, I see it pulled by black chariots,*
*off — toward the unknown,*
*towards its own quiet abyss.*

# AWAKENING HEART

*Your love wells in me:*
*here is the moment in which it stifles me*
*then there is the hour your violent tide washes over me*

*all else in the day is a form of waiting*

# BURIAL

*I am afraid it is my heart,*
*it contains so much of you,*
*still, it bears so much of our past,*
*it digs for you, burlesques with the end —*
*it seeks the burial*

# DARK ANGEL

## I

*O dark wind,*
*blown from the guardianship of malignancy,*
*you came to me in the night and at once, I am all changed,*
*entirely changed — taken from sinlessness by the hand,*
*drawn in by the mouth, into infinite slumber...*
*where the blackness moves like fog, hurls itself,*
*enters me like future —*
*to know such things is to die.*

*Death-bringer, after tonight, I am half-alive,*
*they have gnawed at my childhood.*
*Before I must face this abandon, hold the night,*
*put me to bed —*
*let me dream one last dream.*

*Let me, forget this which fails to escape me, or,*
*perhaps, if just once — let me remember it another way:*
*the damp flesh, the blurred brawn of man, its gracelessness,*
*its terrible force, its unkindness like that of a hunter —*
*they have their weapons: they who love mortality*
*remind me I am mortal and yet I keep my death*
*and have cheated it, too:*
*awoken, still, before invisible angels, blackened with*
*tenderness, thrown away and unfamiliar, tainted —*
*between the thighs*

*Where I would have become a rose, now I bloom into the midnight*
*like the death of a star, the light of my innocence moves*
*through the dust; consume me, dark angel,*
*I am now made in parts*

## II

*By morning, I sought the formlessness of the sea....*
*the envy which went forth from me: deep in my bloodstream*
*like the olde ways, like ancient darkness, twisted vines of ill will.*
*I looked to the black, great mass with a yearning — to be without*
*shape, without the burden of femininity yet full of grace and ominous —*
*always at once, together in equilibrium before the feet of mankind; its*
*shores, like open gates where life itself arose, grasped all meaning of*
*transformation and roared itself into incarnation with cosmic power —*
*that she would receive me still, before her watery kingdom,*
*though my body be unloved, having been filled with poison,*
*ravished and defiled,*
*defied all description*

*How could I not yearn to be such a force: ignorant of mortality,*
*unbounded by time, existence, weakness? Knowing all consequence,*
*how could I have not been the one to jump at the challenge?*
*O to be shapeless, without weight, adorned in flowing mystery!*
*Mother of all Splendor, soft with peace, how is it that you lose*
*no part of your eternity? You, who is swallowed whole by man, like me,*
*taken from, wronged — yet still, you carry in your belly other worlds...*
*dangerous labyrinths of mystery, whole bodies, myths; the cure of all*
*humanness lies in secrecy in the shadows of your mouth....*

*How is it that both you and I, who bear in us the seed of creation, can*
*live out our lives so unlike one another? I am small, so easily am I diminished*
*but you are vast, deathless....incorruptible. I can only sit at your gate and*
*consider your mettle, the strength of your softness, your invisible magic*

*Braveness, be like the sea,*
*knowing no opposites, be all, a world of ones own, knowing only unity —*
*the oneness of gods, who have taken the clear blue of skies and pressed them*
*gently to your boundless mass — treat me to the wholeness you have known,*
*make of me the unbroken vessel where all things can pass through —*
*terrible beauty, infiltrate....*
*I want to free what grows within me*

*so that my troubles be unseen*

## III

*Take from me my breasts, my empty heart which aches,*
*the frailties in me which softly break into the atmosphere...*

*I am suffering from unspeakable emotion,*
*God's black tears are upon my body.*

*I am ravished, ravished through, to the bone...*
*Creator, take me home...*
*I will hold my own hand.*

# THE HAUNTING

*Thoughts of you,*
*they have their home*

*they swell in me like wounds*

# GODDESS

*You were so beautiful to me then —*
*your soul of light, your wraith-like figure —*
*it was as though I could pass my hand through you,*
*untouchable, unreachable…like that of spirit —*
*but still, your essence pressed to mine, tethered to me,*
*as though I could turn it in my fingers*
*as though it was so much my own*

# HEART'S SONG

*Your name moves through the air...*
*piercing the heart: it blooms, it tears*

# THE CURSE

*You have marked me on the body as your own.*
*You, who always have a way of silencing me, godless you,*
*who stains the skin. Your bite comes — and all slips into*
*the dark again; my body twists in the wind, I bend —*
*to let more of you in.*

*My arms and thighs hold your good gnaw, they clutch at shadows.*

*Nothing has remained and yet, I must confess:*
*I could stay here always — half-way between worlds, to dark sleep —*
*holding to your quiet sphere. Your alabaster hand grazes my own…*

*You are my lover and my death. Only you exist. Only you can change all things.*

*I exist at the end of your knife. I am your leading lady. Your prima ballerina,*
*pointed there — at the end of your knife, always — at your shining knife.*

*I, who no longer bleed like a woman my age should*
*and my hair, as thin as a winter branch, am pale white —*
*what I fear waits in a glass.*

*How dreams can lie!*

# PARADISE

*Darling,*

*I am thrown over you*
*like the dark vault of heaven*
*which lies above us…permanently;*
*like the solitary blackbird*
*that opens its wings in embrace*
*for a moment with the sun.*

# I MUST UNLOVE YOU

*By loving you, I have hurt myself. I love you,*
*I hurt myself — it is the way this tale unfurls.*
*I must find it in me to unlove you:*
*like a wound which closes and heals,*
*like a sun which sets, like the final breath which*
*is swallowed whole by the mouth of Death —*
*I must, I must unlove you.*

# THE DEMON

*Who would hold a demon? Who would bathe and nurse it?*
*and where is it that a creature like me rests its head? I have seen*
*Hell and never once shut my eyes, went blind, just sat like one would*
*at a table and turned, from girl to demon, absorbing evil, bruising —*
*slipping from the world like time, as though I was never there, as though*
*I had never come into being, small, wizened and brittle, with bones that*
*push towards the dark like knives, never once screaming for help.*

*And still you came, you rose like mist and your presence was all. You walked,*
*far, you let me stay there in your wings, took from me my rope,*
*pulled me from the edge.*

*Poor Islander, your throat of spanish moss, your working hands,*
*your lion-thighs — you, who crossed an ocean and stepped into my heart,*
*forbidding sorrow, knowing nothing of such a place — you came like*
*dawn and entered my blood, roaring at shadows, opening your mouth and*
*taking in breaths, demanding life exist where it could not, tearing evil,*
*embracing it, kissing it till it screamed, searing through me, exorcising.*

*I know I must have been terrifying to hold and yet, you held me — you, who was born to love, who was born to take me by the blade of my shoulders and pull from them two wings, bright as stars. No, do not sing to me — I cannot bear to hear your song of blood and sun, I cannot bear your loyalty — it is beautiful and I do not deserve it. I'd weep with a depth to know a second of it. I'd die from it for a kindness this tender stays in the bones, travels through the body, marching, always marching, never ceasing...*

*Still, you'd hold my body if it was thrown into flames, this I know —*
*and if it hung from some gallows, blackened and smoking, you'd burn your hands to get me down. What is it in you that knows no fear? What is it in you that wants me alive? Who is this capable? Who is this beautiful to love me this way,*

*with a love which rises from the dead?*

# BURIALS

# FANG & CLAW

*To destroy myself, to erase myself, to hide away…*
*to grow fang and claw and fur to keep one safe,*
*to crawl on all fours, closer to the grounds —*
*away from mankind, away from their teeth…*
*that is what I need,*
*that is all I have ever needed.*

# BLOOD SISTERS

*Before me stood a twin: a shared body, two heads;*
*a joy like no other and a sorrow much darker.*

*The body was theirs, they said...when it was sick,*
*they both endured and when it was well, they both were queen.*
*But the hands, they said — the hands were argued over*
*for hands are seperate things, they said, hands can do things.*

*In Joy's, she held a transculent orb and in it, the world spun —*
*microscopic peaks, small circling birds, bays and oceans,*
*paper boats which glided across the orb, gleaming and gold.*

*In Sorrow's, she held a scythe, as thin and as long, as dark as*
*strands of hair. A scythe adorned with blue veins. She liked to*
*grip it tight for it was then blood would drain and she loved to be emptied.*

*They walked towards me, blue and yellow, the color of a bruise.*

*And Joy said, "at the heart of the world, deep within, is gold."*
*And Sorrow said, "but the heart is first a thing of blood."*

*and from their shared belly drifted a blood filled egg.*

*I opened my mouth and was fed.*

*Iron. Copper. Rust. Salt.*
*I shut my eyes to make the moment last.*

*"Blood is this life and only this life," they said, "after this world, there is no blood, no salt to taste. Endure its bitterness, make it last — for*
*eventually from the heart are born gold skies,*
*surely you can take on her storms."*

# FORSAKEN ME

*I hurl it into the air:*
*"I am alone. I am alone."*

*and all my hurt take flight,*
*all my hurt — ablaze within me*

# RUIN

*Ruin,*
*the unfathomable jolt of the gods,*
*which plunges us from our understanding*
*and twists us into our purpose...*
*Oh,*
*to see again*
*from the slits of tearful eyes*

*out of the ash,*
*with a greater hunger*

# SLEEP & DREAMS

*I must remind myself:*
*how merciful is life to grant me sleep*
*and dreams —*
*to forget, for a moment,*
*my quiet and solitary existence*

# SEAWARD

*At any hour of the day, I am wandering through my own solitude —*
*writing like a woman who has died, between heaven and earth,*
*the places in between. My dream-like solitude — always hungry, always*
*panting out with its long tongue, ruining insides with its white horn.*
*It is my deep sky object, my underwater realm and beneath my skin,*
*the moving shadow of my bone.*

*If you asked me now what could contain such elaborate loneliness,*
*to you I would hurl some page, some shaking paper —*

*and from me, you'd have in your hand a woman, shrouded in black,*
*pale arms reaching towards the sky, seaward and the sea shouts back.*

# THE UNDER

*I knew desire the moment I came into the world.*
*My half-lit desire, my love for shadows…*
*I seek them with a lust for I know Death cannot harm me —*
*it is life which is full of risk and malignity.*

# ASUNDER

*In me, a division of self,*
*a persisting strangeness…*
*the first which longs to blossom*
          *and the other which begs to grow dim*

*I am*
*coming apart these days…*

*I have torn my heart asunder*

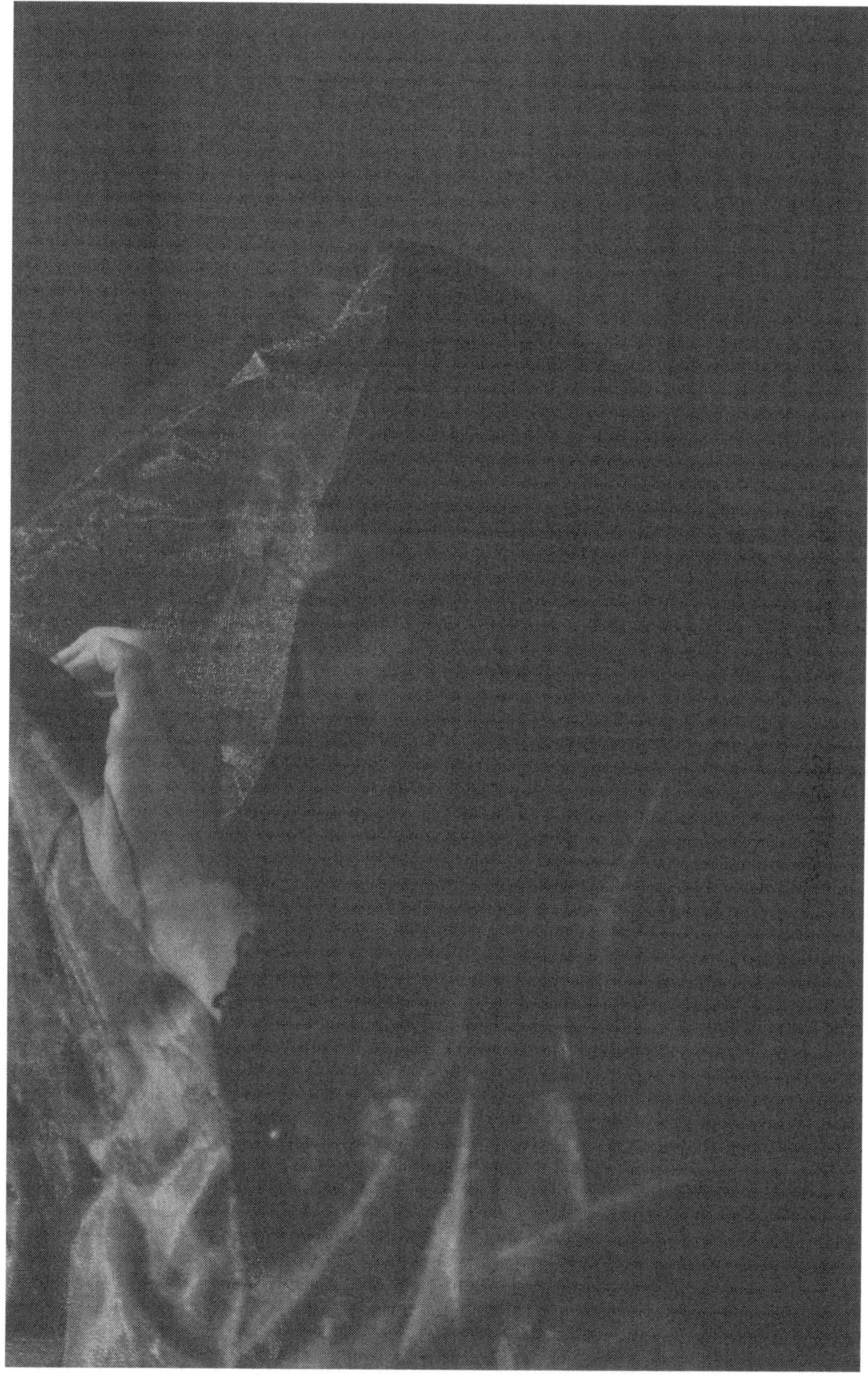

# EVE

*It seems now that Death*
*does not happen all at once on some day, but*
*throughout our day…it seems to mingle between*
*time, like little filaments — delicate and strange,*
*conjoined to the air…*
*Yes, now it seems to be in all things and*
*always at once — is pressed to us…*
            *like the end pages of a book, memories of*
*lost love, the burial of an old self — the final chord.*

# THE DISQUIET

*It is poetry*
*which takes from me my suffering —*
*it stills the disquiet in me.*
*It breathes again where I have breathed.*
*It loves again what I have loved.*

# A NOTE

*I have no desire to know where my poetry will get me.*
*I write because something calls, something jostles —*
*it moves in me like boiling water, it dwells in me like*
*unseen future. It is a knock upon my door, I answer.*

# THE VEIL

*This, you must know first:*
*that I am a creature of elaborate pain —*
*a motherless, fatherless creature*
*shadowed in robes, veiled in black...*
*and that when I write,*
*it is my mother I have found and*
*when I create, it is my home of fire I have built*

# MAUSOLEUM

*My solitude I guard and together we are still as night.*
*I stand, a statue startled into being, covered in my shawl of white gossamer web, spinning my wide net, cutting down all that lives.*

*"I am the loneliest girl in the world," I thought — but no, that isn't true. Most days that is what I want to believe but in the dark of me, in a small and metal room in my heart, I know the truth:*
*my loneliness I choose. I choose it everyday.*

*I walk through its mausoleum doors and they swing, they open without effort, they creak, scratching against the grounds. Down my path, my dress leaves a stain to keep the others at bay. Grit and worm and blood.*

*I make myself within its walls — with an impossibly long nail, I fork out its grey and ancient brick so the sound tells of my presence. Just for me.*
*I must hear a sound to know I am still alive, even in my most interior world. I must drop something to the grounds, must tell a tale, must make a noise...like a ghost trapped in a parlor, turning on table lamps, throwing the roses — passing, as if through the air, moving through dust.*

*I withdraw, I withdraw — it is my law.*

# OBLIVION

*from the journals*

*As a poet, I have been cursed with desire: to immortalize all things — music and rhyme, the running bath water, the ash of the day before, the shadow which swings, the bruising darkness, the beating heart — the found wholeness of being.*
*I do not and have never belonged. I have been alien since birth.*

*I have a courage for the strange...for the most strange. I fear that I am infinite and endless loneliness, streaming in an eternal road, unending — seeing no exit from such fated solitude, such exquisite loneliness.*

*I write and I write and still, most things I save in my chest — blooming, growing red, like bullets through the heart.*

*I have nothing —*

*except my books, for whom I bleed willingly...*
*and an invisible God whose breath passes through me.*

# SERPENS

*To touch the skin... the high hip, womanly frame,*
*the body which rests heavy on the earth,*
*weighed down by things which have caused it shame,*
*burdened by time, by malevolence, by talk of supposed truth —*
*to hold the darkness to it, the heavy mist of darkness...*
*to watch it cascade along the body like the smoke of cauldrons*
*to not challenge it and without difficulty, accept its falsehood*
*when coiled in the belly lives pure desire, the residual power of man,*
*the cosmic body...bestowed with unjust and everlasting curse:*
*sentenced to bite the dust for all eternity, to slither upon the grounds,*
*moving in the underground, in the blackness of time, between realms,*
*roaming where all of life was new —*
*the sun was new, the seas were new, unaware that it was*
*possessed by dark things....To hold the darkness to it, to blame it....*
*to misunderstand it... to deface it and forget its divinity,*
*that is to know lies*

*Touch the skin, cradle it, see it with both eyes...*
*see how its structure is so much of your own,*
*mistaken, unclothed, in search of continual rebirth*
*evenly now, touch the body...*
*a girl bound to darkness*

I AM

RAVAGED, BUT SPIRITED

DAMAGED BUT STILL DESERVING

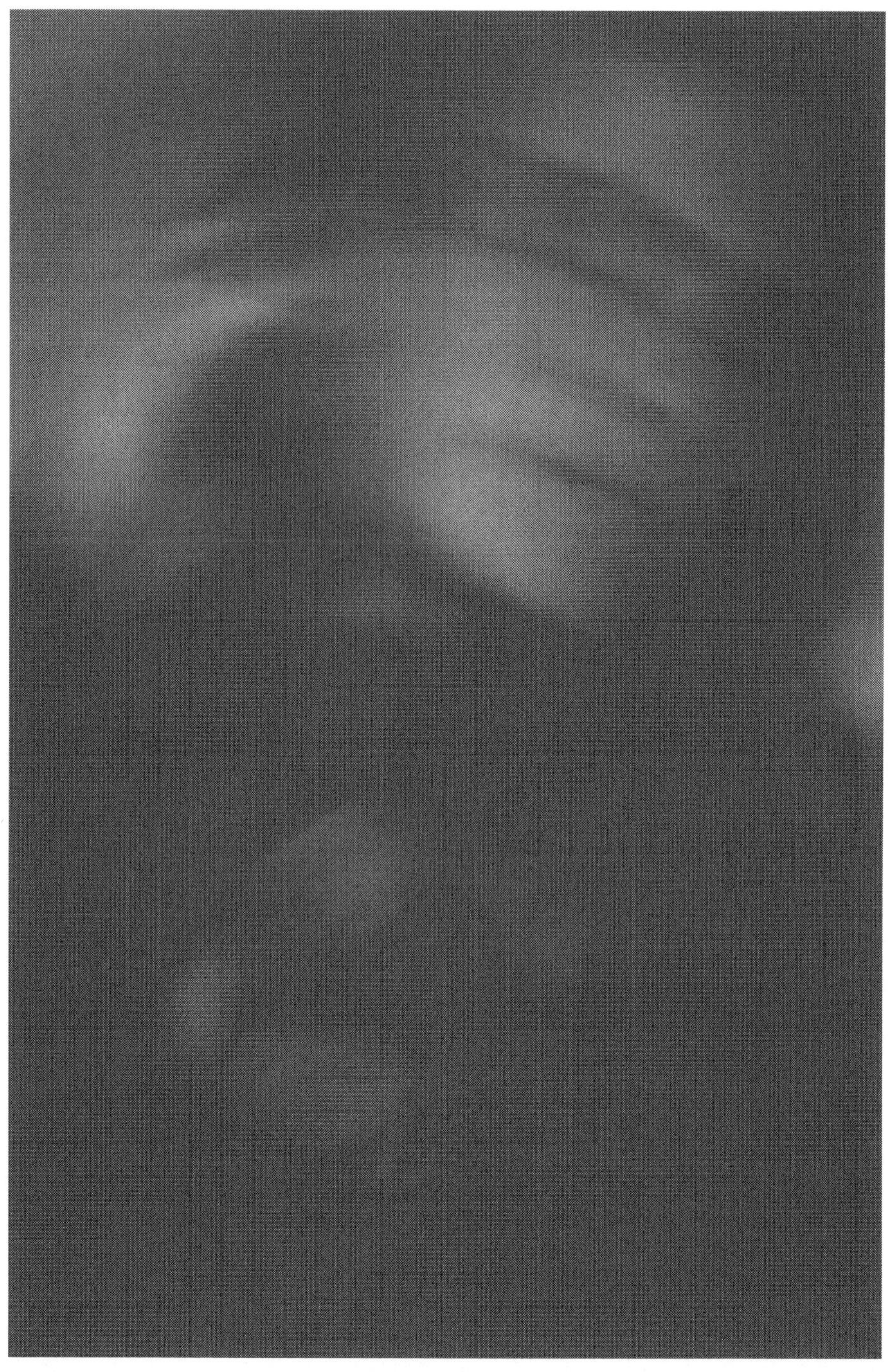

# OUR INMOST CHAMBER

*To be sad is to, almost, experience a moment*
*of paralysis — to be caught up within the*
*stillness of ones own space, disarmed — like*
*witnessing something unknown, something*
*silent, something which brings to a standstill the*
*workings of time and*
*reaps dominion over our inmost chamber*

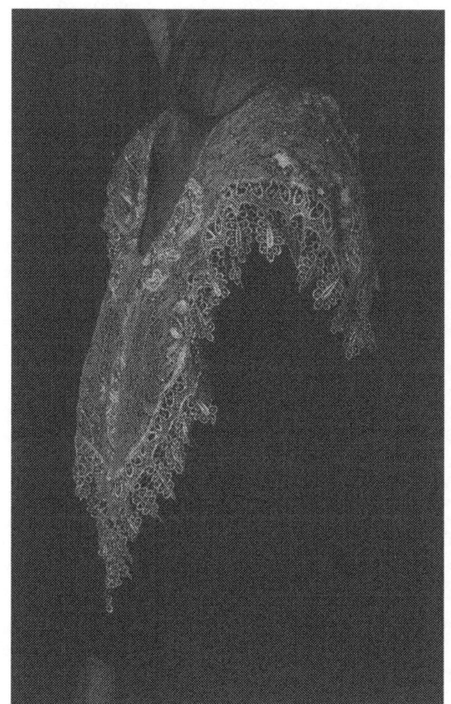

# PINNACLE

*I have existed in solitude —*
*it has its seat in my body...*
*it is more alive than my own sorrowful thoughts,*
*more alive than the shadow*
*which hangs on me like a dress*

# CATHEDRAL

*This heart is a cathedral.*
*Widows, ghosts and lovers sit and sing*
*in the dark, arched marrow of me.*

# DAMNED

*All of me is damned.*
*From earliest beginnings,*
*my fate has been solitude —*
*elegant solitude, elegant loneliness.*
*I let it walk into me as into a cathedral,*
*down its aisle — wedding bells sound*
*in the secret place of my heart*

# LILITH

*Dearest Lilith,*
*shadow sister who, coiled in the womb, lives unseen —*
*I dreamt you were floating face down in a black sea. You were immersed.*
*Gazing, I suppose, into the many eyes of Death, into another dark — the one*
*from which you became; your isolated, private dark. I screamed out to you*
*from my boat. I called you "sister." I asked you to show yourself to me but you*
*did not turn, you did not flinch — you did not answer, all that was: my own*
*echoing across the black sea and sky which merged and showed no distinction.*
*I pulled you from Mother's dark embrace and you allowed me, you did not*
*fight me. I pulled you up towards my boat. I held you as though to feed you*
*upon my breast. My arms blackening with the trail of your body. Your dead*
*limbs heavy with the weight of the world, your dark wet wings, two-ton,*
*with the smell of burning upon them. I turned you around to me. I feared you*
*would resemble me. You did. My very face was your own face. All of my ugly,*
*all my unclean, all of my sorrow, all of my hate — there, crystallized upon*
*your face. I opened your mouth and there sat all my lies. I looked for your*
*hands and rain began to fall. Our boat swaying upon the black sea.*

*Stay here, in the cut out of my boat, my swaying, wooden boat. I am you.*
*We will wait till morning comes, surely it will come — as all has already come*
*for us, surely morning too will come.*

# DARK MEMENTO

*With all that I know,*
*and all the seriousness I have collected,*
*still, there are parts of me which beg*
   *to be pulled into the mouth of sorrow,*
    *to sleep inside the hole of her insecurity*
     *to be*
         *dragged out the other side,*
*for just a glimpse, an understanding...*
*to taste again,*
*the weakness of mortal heartbeat*

# DARKNESS REIGN

*It has always been darkness*
*which hands me the brush, the pen —*
*all the instruments of creation*

# PRISM

*I do not want to stand before you a mum,*
*hushed and still, an emblem of inaction*

*I have endured all desire,*
*with its intervals of silence and its full-bodied blackness,*
*I have picked up the shards of its subtle nuances*
*and grown apart,*
*like a prism, I have isolated the aching into*
*infinite spectrum*

*I do not want to simply stand before you now,*
*I want to unravel,*

*the silence begs to rupture*

## GONE AWAY

*You are gone now and there is no reaching you…*
*yet still, you cloak me — you hover like shadow,*
*here the place we are destined for:*

*you can survive in my heart*

## THE GALLOWS

*Sorrow, like an arrow,*
*flies into the dark atmosphere of my heart —*
*it is caught in my wilderness,*
*pendulous, it hangs from my gallows*

# DREAMLAND

*To me,*
*you came in a dream…*
*it was there I could hold you again*
*it was there, that I could speak to you again*
*and there, between the realm of the undying*
*and the world of the living*

*that I let my heart break twice*

# TRUE LOVE

*From the white bone of my frame,*
*to the even paler tissue which veils me —*
*there lives poetry,*
*my whole existence*

# SWOLLEN

*It is a beautiful thing — for once,*
*to be swollen, but by other words,*
*by non-words: to be swollen by love*
*which seeks not words but touch,*
*which does not lie*

# YEMAYA

*We came to Yemaya and from behind her black veil,*
*she shouted — a raging, threatening, immortal thing.*
*We trudged forth towards her body. It was midnight*
*and from afar, she possessed us —spat at us, cursed us,*
*pushed us back, but we kept on, at war with her winds:*
*"to the body, to the body," we said,*
*"to the darkness within darkness,*
*there are prayers to be sung."*

*At night, Yemaya cries. She grows hands and leaps, claps,*
*spits, damning the moon. She screeches like a banshee and drowns*
*her children.*

*There we were at the dark shore of her mouth,*
*her black mist hatched forth at us, beckoning us,*
*like the nativity of a thousand wet serpents,*
*she came alive — a faceless power.*

*We had our offerings. Our sweet melon. Our tough sugar.*
*I dreamt the ocean floor was a tongue, wet and covered in salt,*
*rough with sand, spitting pearl — starved for sweet, honey, nectar.*
*These I brought to Yemaya: sweet round, blue-green melon.*

*"Yemaya, there are wounds in my mind which make me think evil.*
*O, I have done evil. I have thrown it forth, before me, into the air*
*I breathe. I had taken it, too, in the lungs. My heart is mummified,*
*blood-streaked."*

*and her wave rose to meet me, like the opening of a thousand black flowers,*
*taking from me my sweet, my unholy, all my untrue.*

# WARRIOR

*Watch me.*
*I will go to my own Sun.*
*And if I am burned by its fire,*
*I will fly on scorched wings.*

BESIDE ME ALWAYS,

A KINGDOM OF SPIRIT;

INSIDE OF ME,

A HAUNTED HOUSE.

# THE ROAD

*Inside myself, I've seen a Hell —*
*a road so thick with blood, unspeakable violence, beauty and tragedy,*
*so thick you could take it in by the mouth, like cream or black roe,*
*and know the wounds hidden in my jaw.*

*This is my road, I say, down in the dark of me, a part of me sits like a*
*hunched beast, where red clouds fall like terrible angels and night, with*
*its distant growl invades, like a secret, like cold wind — thrashing like*
*an angry god, never to feel the sun…*

*I was given pale soles, tough and tender, padded like a cat to walk upon*
*its grounds and claws, to push open its high gate of bone, two eyes, never to blink,*
*to watch, from the bone door, as wounds bloom from the concrete like new moons,*
*speaking, swelling up, more whole than before, repairing themselves.*

*I put flowers on my body, like they do for the dead and walk down my*
*own aisle. The dead have no shame and this is my road: adorned with*
*fountains of blood, hiding all light, its floor strewn with soft hearts, cut in*
*two, speaking to their halves, echoing, always — histories of a love that disfigures.*

*I walk down my road and everything bleeds, all is crying out into me like mangled things.*
*I scream with them for I am their queen. Our blood and our wanting streams*
*towards the air, like a choir of angels, like violins seeping fire, twisting out our pain,*
*a thousand voices, knotting together, kicking up the dark, carrying our death.*

*This is my road, I say;*

*and in it, I lie in my long hair, deep within myself — as though I am my own offspring,*
*as though I am a closing night flower, into my world of crimson and ice…*
*a pale butterfly, ominously tender, bleary as if underwater — floating in a wet cloak,*
*passing through Hells, screaming into the silence, holding nothing back.*

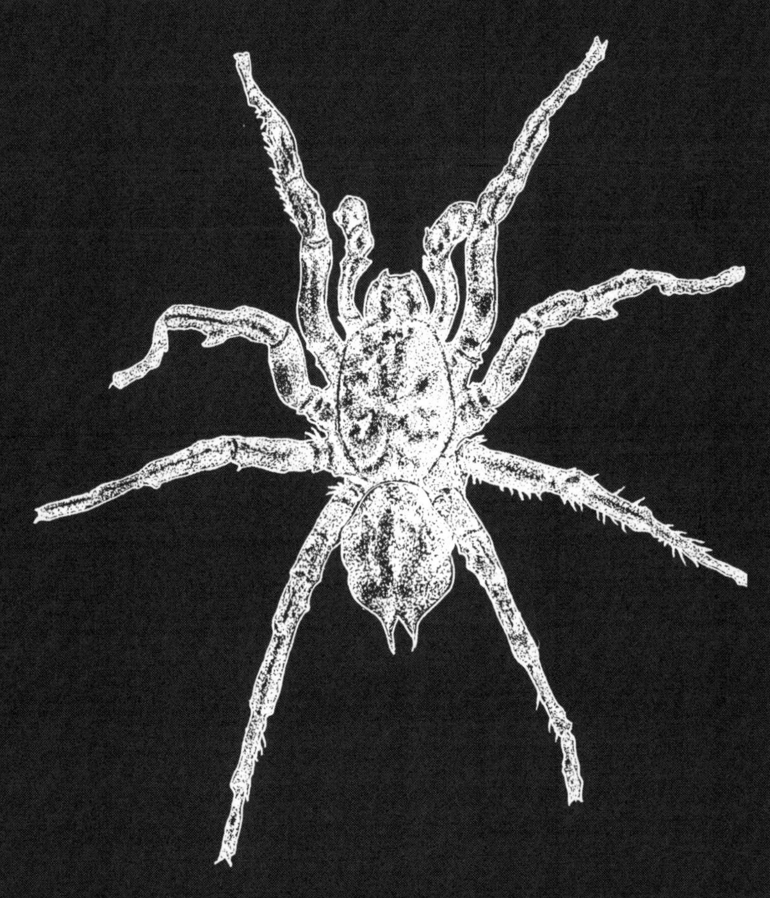

# UNDERWORLD

*She who walks the floors of Hell*
*finds the key to the gates of her own Heaven,*
*buried there like a seed.*

# THE SPELL

*Upon being born, a rippling pain*
*to touch the farthest moon, to be soft and close to death,*
*weary like a petal on the protruding arm of Aquarius,*
*to weep in the depths of her cascading sea...*
*with shining scales: a mermaid corpse.*

*It filled me — to dream impossibilities, like a spell*
*which takes hold, it loomed until it was my whole world;*
*and yet it was my pain, and I am greedy with my pain,*
*wringing it out of me like innocence, virginity —*
*all which belongs to a young girl is fated: a devil's bride.*

*I slept inside such longings and was joyous, carried*
*myself over unimagined bridges, heavy as a rope, filled*
*with black and invisible treasures, with blood and wanting.*
*To sleep is to die, to die is to dream — a life sharp and cruel*
*with wreaths for eyes, hidden in their own jungles, sheathed*
*in their own wild laws for a dream has teeth and eats of our*
*fruit, our thick blood fruit and makes our beds red seas.*

HALF OF ME, FOR GROWTH

THE OTHER,FOR DECAY

# VICTORIA

*Because nothing about me was simple,*
*I yearned for simplicity…*
*O, to be unknown, unborn —*
*to start again, simply,*
*out the rib of man and into*
*the divine body of the unafraid….*

*yet, the ways in which I have become*
*never sought simplicity but*
*beckoned for intricacies to slay me*

*and so, I trust the elaborate plane I grow into strangely,*
*slouched and warped*

*I trust the process*

# MELANCHOLIA

*Melancholia — a spell, a witch, death-like sleep.*
*Each of us, traveling in her long black arms —*
*quietly devoured, falling to the Earth unguided...*

*until we are disfigured, limb to limb, reborn —*
*turned from ash to firebird.*

# BLACK IN HAND & HEART

*See how all that is dead is at rest...*
*all is aching and suffering until its final moment,*
*until darkness encloses it in its misty trench — its*
*sighs rise from the grounds, like the undead, it wanders —*
*settling in slow decay, in passing time, in waning moons.*

*Look here, now, it is asleep in me —*
*it is always asleep, this foreigner I have loved;*
*this which only dreams comes to me in the hour*
*like foresight, like premonition, like destiny.*
*My love is always here and longs to be awakened,*
*like a pyre of once fledging roses —*
*at once, it both withers and grows, it turns, it yawns.*

*Patient, interior death...black in hand and heart,*
*you take form in your sleep, you are always growing, winding*
*like a child in the womb, like a serpent moving in its leathery egg.*
*I am your egg. I am brooding.*
*I am keeping you warm and safe and tucked away.*
*When will I discover you? What shape shall you make of me, potter?*
*Where, first, will you break me with your long pale tooth?*

*You, who march and swim and mold, make your slow waves upon my face.*
*Surely someday when you wake, it will be my time to be at rest.*

# KURGARRA, GALATUR

*In the Underworld there live two beings, their names with no translation,*
*wandering small black flies — unseeable, unable to be captured...*
*unique beings which can only be felt: music, prayer, breath and breeze.*

*I have reached for them and they disperse — smoke, vapor, black matter.*
*Surely, they are made up of multitudes. I have called to them and they echo.*

*They fly, they crawl — stalking, lifting the dust, turning off my porch light.*
*When I am mourning something catches fire and they slip under my door.*

*When I am weeping, a mirror materializes before me and I watch it come into being.*
*In horror, I watch my flesh burn oxblood and break open like a wound.*

*The girl on the other side does as I do: where my skin grows hot, hers does too.*
*When I am grieving, my wailing is pulled into tomorrow — heard, one after the other,*

*like drops of falling rain, slipping expressions of pain.*

*In so many spaces, who out there watches?*

# BLOOD OF THE SEED

*In a dream, Persephone kisses my long, thin spine with wet blooded lips,*
*(the bit of a fruit once devoured) and says, "a girl who falls through my*
*roof is safe with me for I know her kind and nothing will touch her."*
*Yet everything clings to me — and I am always humid like the air, coming*
*out of her river, again and again, drops of dark water draw on me a coat,*
*a film reel on repeat.*

*She asks me to sit, in her chair of black ore, and she will tell me of longing,*
*of desires and cravings, of how innocence washes off.*

*"I know the story," I say, "I know it well. I know everything except*
*what was happening to you, down here, in the dark depths of the world.*
*Only you know that story."*

*They say Persephone's eyes change like the seasons, multicolored —*
*hyacinth, burnt sap, a basket of apples, frosted by nightfall,*
*but now they were as fresh as new blood, eclipsed by a wound.*

*"This story hurts to tell," and her hair, which touched the ground, as*
*long as her dress, rose like an arrow, a flock of black birds.*

*She dove down to me like a swan and kissed me again, placed her ear*
*to my heart and said, "there is a secret room in your heart, in there lives*
*a little girl, she has not died for she is immortal. The girl in a woman never dies.*
*She knows the story, too.*

*Write it.*

*For it is my own story."*

# SUMMONING

*All this world walks through me now.*
*I will not mourn my dead.*
*I will bring them out. I will celebrate them.*
*They will rush out towards life,*
*like blood from a cut.*

# UNDERWATER

*I have drunk the milk of the poem,*
*placed my mouth upon the mouth*
*of a once drowning girl, taken in her ocean salt,*
*brought her back from the dead —*
*a dark flower unfurls in my throat —*
*never to close.*

# THE FRUIT OF SOLITUDE

*In each of us, two lives —*

*one of light, the white whole milk of life...*
*from it, you drink and work and grow and write of your becoming*
*as though you have slid down the blade of life, unscathed...*
*as though you have cheated death and are unwounded, whole,*
*intact with your flesh which is dying — and your shadow*
*which follows you secretly all the days of your life.*

*Your other life, your true life — ghostly and known to you alone*
*is darker than your darkness, is the hanging fruit of your solitude...*
*and so too you eat of this fruit and are made whole by its thickness,*
*its juice is drawn like blood from a vein; outpouring, it floods the hour,*
*floods the mouth and you become alive elsewhere — and what was once*
*submerged comes forth like buried seeds. Now you are most alive, here,*
*in your quiet and private hour which weighs on you heavily, dangerously,*
*which integrates you with something unnamed, something sinister, something in vain.*

*It is this life, always beneath and behind you, inside you,*
*it is this life which reigns.*

# MONSTRUM

*It is the monstrous thing I love —*
*the hunchback, the demon, the conjoined twins.*
*For had I not been born and touched first by ugliness,*
*which one of you would love me?*
*Who here would read my poetry?*

*I will write for ugliness.*

*I will write for monsters and demons, for serpents,*
*for giants and dwarfs, ogres and ghouls.*

*I will write for the monstrous curse I wear*
*which has turned to blood within me…*
*for the curse which makes me love these things…*
*for the curse which makes me see it is they*
*who most resemble me.*

# METAMORPHOSIS

*Metamorphosis,*
*this you must already know,*
*how you have your place between my silences...*
*between and within —*
*the deep breathing wilderness*

*of my own selfhood*

# PALE DEATH

*Each day death crawls into my body:*
*cutting through, with talon and tooth —*
*falling from above, with scythe and shroud,*
*reaching for me, tying me to dreams,*
*luring me — who cannot deny such angel.*

# THOROUGHBRED

*Before my smallness,*
*which is pulled to pieces by mankind,*
*here is my larger body — I have seen it,*
*I have held it in the night upon my breast,*
*it is sown with the fragrance of the Promised Land:*
*unable to be destroyed, everlasting upon the sea which softens —*
*it calls from that place, that shadowy place, that hazy place…*
*in the wake of my own heart.*
*I have come to this place and have chosen my sorrow*
*and my sorrows took off their masks — showed themselves*
*to me as shrouded joys — without them, I am tousled:*
*a vulture upon the golden field of being*
*with no flight nor food to nourish itself*

*It is that which has brought me sorrow that fills me now with joy:*
*it was my homelessness, my abandon, my unrequited love.*
*It was my insane hopes and my fragilities which purged me*
*and still purge me: they cascade from my mouth,*
*burning the throat, infinitely vaster, with light and space.*

*My sorrows, proud to play their part, I have thanked them.*
*I have danced with them and shared food with them —*
*having worked themselves into my bones, I greet them with joy.*
*I kiss their hands and surrender to them —*
*for what is beyond them,*
*obscured and ill defined,*
*carries me to the terrible, engulfing,*
*majestic desert of my soul…*

THE ONLY WAY TO RELEASE THE
FEELING OF CAPTIVITY
WITHIN THE UNKNOWN IS TO
WALK THROUGH THE UNKNOWN.

# BRUJA

*The darkness in a woman is such that,*
*stripped of our sight, we must feel our way through it —*
*we crawl, we enter her circles of Hell*
*until we sympathize with her sorrow,*
*until we learn from her rage.*

# DEAREST

*Dearest spirit, take me by the heart —*
*back! back! to the time before,*
*when I was a man, or mother,*
*fallen angel or rogue…*

*Dearest spirit, take me back —*
*back! back! to the time before,*
*I want to see all the places I have died.*

## SEVEN HELLS

*I have asked for my Heavens, my Hells*
*and between my heart,*
*composed the language*
*which sets them apart.*

## BOUND BY BIRTH

*Had you not already existed within me from the*
*moment of my birth —*
*how should I have known you*
*or felt your rich harmony upon me now?*

# IMMORTELLE

*Sewn together:*
*my humanness and my immortality.*
*Together they hang, trading places,*
*like sun and moon,*
*like pendants in the sky.*

# BLOOD MOON RISING

*Each day I come up, blood-streaked and bruised,*
*dirtier than before — my black wings of dusk,*
*my heels of dark fire*
*and know the kingdom I rule.*

*Each day it is my duty to know my own mind —*
*its dark fantasies and its buried genius. To know the*
*hidden language of my soul — to excavate it from some*
*ruined place, some battered place in me that I must take back.*

*My Patron Dark Goddess asks me what must die in me*
*and I say, "that which is untrue — break it from me,*
*destroy it with your merciless hand."*

*I tell her if I am to lose or forget who I am,*
*I will wane, I will waste away, I will pass into nothing.*

*Each day I rise and have my seed, my key.*

*Upon my head, I place my own crown — this I give to myself*
*because it is all I must do, because I cannot help but respect*
*myself and my future.*

*My kingdom, I know. My kingdom, I guard.*

*To my kingdom, I am true.*

# WITH HER, I SEE A FLAME

*I give my life to poetry —*
*who has never asked me to tell her*
*but begs me to take her by the dark arm and show her.*
*Together we journey, I and my beloved;*
*my eyes are hers, my hands are hers,*
*my very limbs belong to her.*

*We are one chamber —*
*sisters, dancing in the cathedral of our voices,*
*joined in utero,*
                *in the beautiful darkness.*

# THE DEEPENED SOUND

*I chose you*
*long before I experienced you here,*
*you, who is overflowing with both color and sound —*
*and I will chose you again,*
*between this world and the bounty of our next world*

*until our eyes go softly towards their decay,*
*until our bodies illuminate into the atmosphere —*
*where the thread of our spirit is fastened, our eternal home*

# MARINER

*On a day like today, I fell from the earth and dreamt I was a man,*
*from my heart stuck brittle shell, blanched barnacle, lasting sorrow,*
*cutting through like knives. This is what happens when you love —*
*your house, it dies and you turn from flesh to stone while you're still standing.*
*You don't know when or how it happened but in your mouth, the taste is thick:*
*of metal and exhaust and the bitterness of the sea, it snags the heart,*

*crawls out over the blood: tears and tears, salt and salt.*

# THE OATH

*To my body, I give the oath*
*I look at her tissue, the river of her throat*
*the mortal flesh which houses her spell work,*
*the mysterious form she has taken on*
*the wounds she has healed herself*

*My body, who is far truer than any poem*
*to my body,*
*I give and I receive*

# THE DARK ART

*There cannot be a passion much greater than this —*
*it wells up in me, makes my heart ache...*

*until my eyes brim with water,*
*until my lashes grow dark*

# THE BIRD

*A woman who stands by death's side behaves as a bird*
*and death does not grieve her for she has seen him.*
*Skin, blue-black and hiding all light — for once you*
*have seen him, it is you who knows things and the world*
*sloughs off like ash, like leaves in a thoughtless winter.*

*Death makes it colorless, death makes it tasteless.*

*You catch a glimpse of him and it is you who now belong*
*to two worlds and you move between them, too fast to see.*
*You are emptied into him, chasing him in your sleep,*
*moving each day as though through water: you are his*
*secret, his foliage of fairy moss — you bathe in his water,*

*you saturate in his dust and maintain the wings he stitched*
*into you the moment you first saw him and were turned from*
*girl to bird. It was then Death swooped the known world from you*
*with a waxen hand and you too learned to plummet through a then*
*unknown world, divining, with your massive winged shoulders, your*
*black shining back, your beak of bone — your other life.*

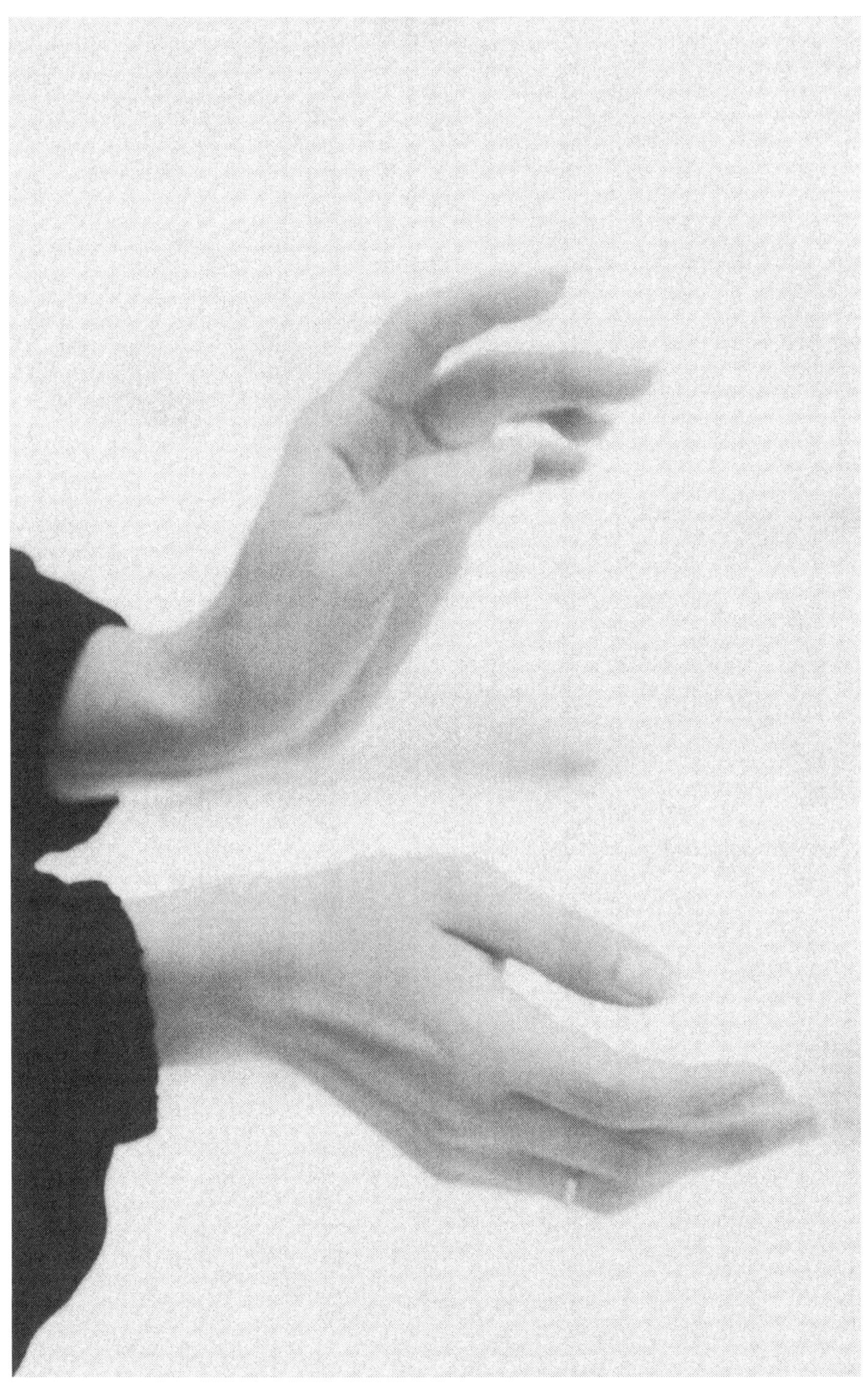

## STILLNESS

*Stillness,*
*the wide-eyed stillness, blinks and at once,*
*we are awakened — softly, gently…*

*into the mystery of the spaces we breathe*

## GHOST LIGHT

*Blood seeps from all shadows, it collects at the root,*
*mingles like mouths joined and as if in grief, holds*
*to what was once near — a ghost light.*

# UMBRA

*In the shade, I spend my life —*
*in continuous travel between living and dead;*
*see here, my heart of metal, my black wings,*
*stretched out on the grass…*
*drawn down on the ground*
*like dark waves that recede*

# IN THE ETHER

*For so long I have considered the lengths of our affinity,*
*our permanence and our likeness which to me,*
*seem tethered by immaculate reason —*
*your naked heart fastened to my own*
*each heartbeat, as one, together between life spans,*
*intended for unearthing that which is*
*beyond — and yet within my knowing*

*I had wondered how I, to whom this past belonged,*
*could pass into the invisible world, to see your face*
*for the first time and know you*

*Unformed and most desiring, I had*
*tested the realness of your unproclaimed genius,*
*sought to display you, make you visible to me,*
*clawed at the fruit of consciousness, the world of your body,*
*flung you into darkness where still, you survived by*
*the vast reservoirs of your love, whose stream is*
*absolute and unending, filled with an inbred brilliance*

*It was then, by intuitive knowing,*
*by my secret self, you came to me, omitting the precision*
*of being, the completeness of my own*

*Where once I had believed I carried in me a single heart,*
*now, the veil which had been drawn down upon me*
*moved upwards, ascending by air and now,*
*it is everywhere that you echo before me,*
*like a gospel, your song of trueness, full of breath,*
*the deep-breathing rawness, the gust around and within*
*my unripe spirit — where all of your unfolding power exists*

*In deep thought, in the quiet hours of my own wilderness,*
*I call your name, I move upwards, I wait inside your white realm*
*and you show yourself to me with a swiftness*

*Forgetting, for a moment, that I am a suffering being*
*by this reunion of the awakened and immortal mirror of self*

*I have memorized your face, my eternal frame, seated*
*in the ether, in the air, in the generous space of purpose —*
*the meeting by which I am made transformed with endless vision*
*with insight of the interior guide, rescued and preserved*
*by you, the perfected and farseeing twin of my design*
*who holds the bond and evidence of my spirit,*
*by you, who is my tie to the heavens*

# WITH MY DEAD

*My spirits dress, wandering — a walking dress,*
*a ghost in mourning, wailing through the parlour.*
*Each day I grow increasingly weary with the ways*
*of the living: their new age declarations, their hunger,*
*their ever growing noses, their greed and cliches —*
*trite and old and lacking in genius.*

*and I withdraw — to my paintings, to my books, to*
*my poetry, I withdraw. I go in, through, to the*
*black doors of my heart, to my phantasmal world*
*where no one can touch me — except maybe a shadow,*
*a spirit, something of Other…the ghost of a girl that is*
*me, the me that is most true…hovering there, wandering*
*through my own misty heavens with my dead and my dreams.*

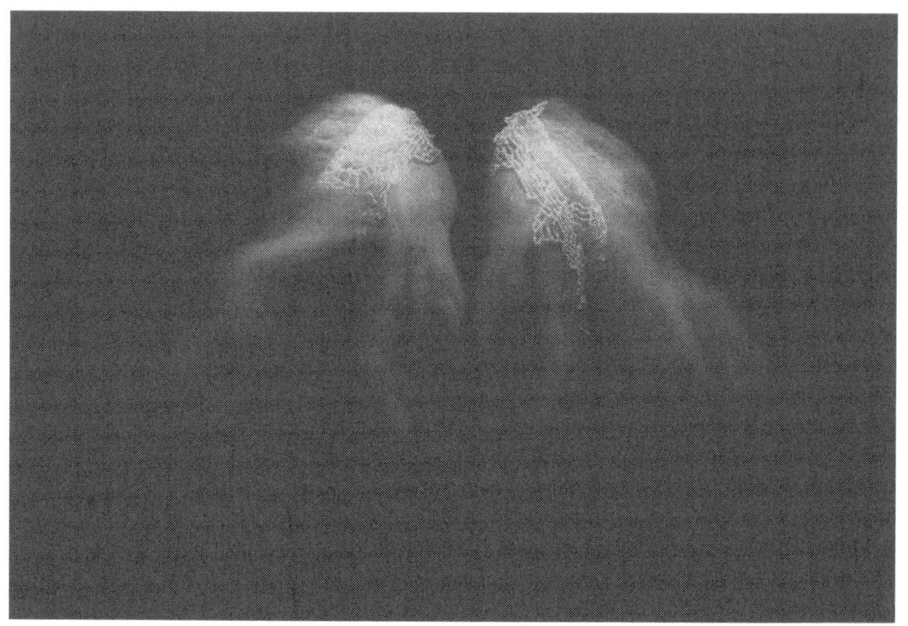

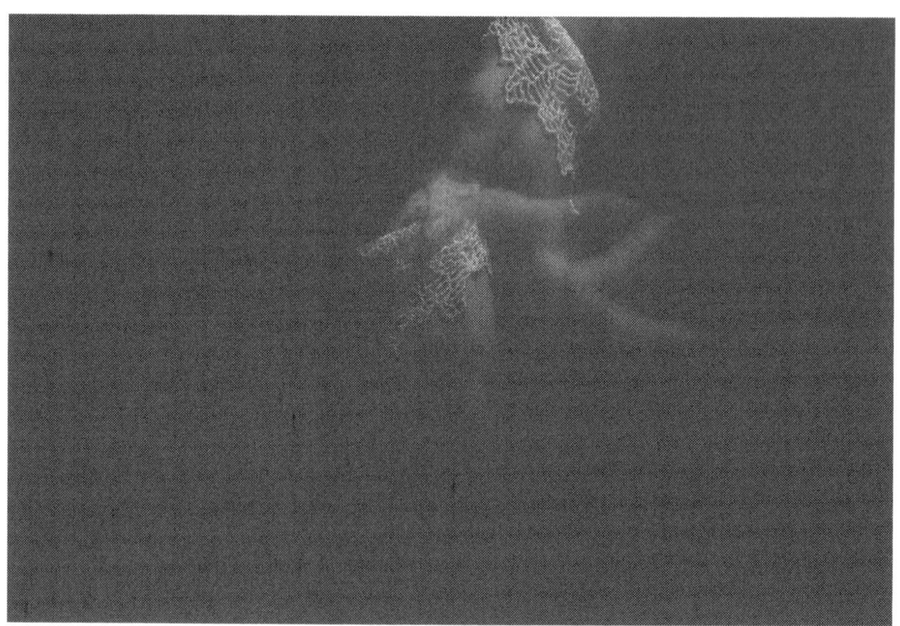

# QUIETLY, LIKE AN EYE

*Seeing the bottom — it is something you learn. The quietude*
*kicks up the dark and shadows hang like long thin arms, like*
*loose black hair, they touch the ground like black gowns.*

*Several fields deep, this non-earth turns black quickly, wetly*
*and dreams no longer live — they turn to whispers and marry*
*the tongue: they swell in the mouth like dark curls underwater.*

*Down there, you are company, another wound within wounds*
*and the air, it bends because it is made of the departed — lost*
*things: hard-edged and cruel as shards which pass into the skin.*

*You walk, a corpse, and its gates seem endless. It is your own*
*unarmed war and the you that was you whorls behind, a thing*
*that rustles — a paling butterfly, shining quietly like an eye.*

# GENESIS CRIES

*I, who was once all quietness and innocence,*
*stand at the mouth of Hell and lunge forward*
*for in my heart lives a solemn passion,*
*an inbred longing to be thrown through to the hungry doorway*
*of my own spirit*
*and be released of this aching form*

*this girlish form which swells at the waist and at the breast,*
*its billows give way to a heartlessness*
*and while I am all tenderness and beginning,*
*by hallowed reason,*
*I have swallowed whole*
*the*
*sharp unkindness of humanity*

*I am*
*unafraid to passage out into the beyond,*
*(those dark and satiated measures of Otherness)*
*and it is because I have known mercilessness,*
*fast and loose, I am brave enough to dispossess this body,*
*to overthrow it and be without its weakness,*
*I know I was made to leap beyond the bounds of my femininity*
*yes, it is my duty to bear it*
*but before that, it is my duty to be freed of it,*
*to recreate it*

*I can let everything happen to me,*
*I can welcome all things*
*(and if they do not find me, I will go after them)*
*it is then I can pull back the arrow of my unabridged selfhood,*
*and as it makes it way into the void, into the threatening silence,*
*I know that there live angels beneath it which guide my bow*
*and by my faith, I watch it inflame*
*as it ascends into the beyond, so do I*

*If I am to drink the fire of my own fountain,*
*I will and must receive myself in embrace...*
*only then can I awake.*

## NEEDLE & THREAD

*My dark love descends,*
*like needle to thread.*
*Darkness, my needle;*
*my body, the thread.*

## BLACK ROSE

*It was in my flaws,*
*I found a much deeper truth —*
*and it is from them,*
*I bloom: a black rose*

# OPHELIA

*Ophelia floats softly and slowly within us — her irises invisible.*
*Both exorcist and charmer, hybrid of angel and demon.*
*Her twisted frame, a wet black root; her haunted heart,*
*a secret room with many doors — love and passion, tragedy, curse.*

*Death and beauty, thrown together, there in her heart, tangled as a braid.*

*She holds the darkness, bringing it forward, cupping the twilight like water,*
*rippling in soft white hands. She puts flowers on her body and summons her own*
*holy war, sharp and cruel and ready — for descent, departure, raw as the night.*

*She thrashes — through the dead worlds, through all seven gates, bruised as a*
*rosebush, red beads drifting before white cheeks — a beauty which damns.*

*She is Ophelia and she will not leave without her blood seed.*

*I journey into her ocean of throes, learning to see,*
*webbing, twisting, breaking bones — made serpentine,*
*no longer a girl, tasting the fruit of a once sleeping soul,*

*letting loose*
*what begs to remain.*

## SEGOVIA AMIL

*Segovia Amil is a poet, writer and artist living in Venice, California. Her work focuses on the shadow, death and darker elements of the human experience. She reads, writes and performs her poetry and prose at local music and spoken word events in her area. She lives with her partner and three cats.*

*segoviaamilpoetry.com*

28334927R00130

Made in the USA
San Bernardino, CA
27 December 2015